Rights & Risk

A discussion document on
civil liberty in old age

Alison J Norman

First published by the National Corporation
for the Care of Old People, now renamed
Centre for Policy on Ageing,
February 1980.
1st reprint   November 1980
2nd reprint with revised Foreword July 1987
ISBN 0 904139 20 4

Set in Monotype Garamond
Printed and bound in Great Britain by
Anchor Brendon Ltd, Tiptree, Essex.

Centre for Policy on Ageing
25-31 Ironmonger Row
London EC1V 3QP

CENTRE FOR POLICY ON AGEING is formally registered
as The National Corporation for the Care of Old People.
It is a registered charity no. 207163 and a company
limited by guarantee, registered in London no. 440135
at the above registered office.

Contents

The Centre for Policy on Ageing was established in 1947 to promote better services for older people. An independent policy unit, the Centre aims to stimulate informed debate about issues affecting older age groups, to increase awareness of the needs of older people, to formulate and promote policies, and to encourage the spread of good practice. The Centre primarily serves those who are responsible for the planning and implementation of public policy at national and local levels.

Central to its role as a policy-informing body, is the provision of advice and information to professionals and academics with an interest in ageing. The Centre's Information Service fulfils this role by monitoring current research and literature on ageing and running Britain's foremost specialist Library in the field. It is on the basis of this excellent collection that CPA publishes a series of comprehensive reference works, including topical biographies and a directory of social research, along with major reports and policy studies on old age. The Centre's Fieldwork unit maintains an interest in residential care and the needs of housebound and vulnerable elderly people. It is actively involved in initiatives which aim to integrate *all* older people in the community.

Further information about the work of the Centre and the full range of CPA publications can be obtained by sending a large self-addressed envelope to:

Centre for Policy on Ageing
25-31 Ironmonger Row
London EC1V 3QP
Tel: 01 253 1787

Foreword

When CPA came to consider reprinting Rights and Risk two questions were relevant. The first was 'Is what this discussion document has to say about civil liberty and elderly people still true and important?' The second was 'Has so much changed since it was written in 1979 that it is now misleading in factual terms?'

CPA believes that the issues raised in Rights and Risk are still of crucial importance. Although society has become more aware of the need to respect self-determination and offer genuine choice to frail elderly people, actual change has been slow and piecemeal. Indeed, a constant battle now needs to be waged against the pressure to cut resources and levels of service provision. Unless this is done, it is only too likely that in practical terms the independence of frail elderly people will be even more restricted in the 1990's than it was when this report was first published. However, there have been some important developments since the report was first published of which readers should be aware, and these are summarised below.

Changes in the law

The Registered Homes Act 1984[1] gives both power and responsibility to local authorities and health authorities in England and Wales to monitor the quality of care provided in private residential homes and nursing homes, and to refuse initial registration or continued registration to homes which are not deemed to be reaching a sufficient standard. A system of tribunals deals with appeals against their decisions. For the first time, therefore, complainants concerning quality of care in residential care homes have a statutory means of seeking redress. The standard which should be met is set out in Home life: a code of practice for residential care[2]. This code was drawn up by a Working Party convened by CPA at the request of the DHSS. It lays down in some detail what residents have a right to expect in any institution offering longstay care, and is an integral part of the new system. It covers such issues as basic principles of care; admission procedures; privacy and personal automony; financial affairs; terms and conditions of residence; physical facilities; health care; and staffing, as well as giving detailed advice to local authorities concerning their role in managing and inspecting voluntary and private residential care homes. It is very much to be hoped that the local authorities use the code to assess and match the standard of care in the homes which they themselves provide.

Guardianship Orders under Section 7 of the Mental Health Act 1983[3]

This Section of the 1983 Mental Health Act permits adults suffering from mental disorder to be taken into Guardianship if 'it is necessary in the interests of the welfare of the patient or for the protection of other persons that the patients should be so received'. Such an order requires a recommendation from two doctors setting out the nature of the illness and the reason why the order is necessary, plus an application from an approved social worker or the nearest relative of the patient. The nearest relative must in any case be informed as soon as possible and an order is not valid if they object. A Guardianship order gives the appointed guardian (who may be the local authority social services department or any individual approved for the purpose by the local authority) power to require the patient to reside at a particular place; to attend a particular place for the purpose of 'medical treatment, occupation, education or training'; and to give access to any specified person. It does not give authority to manage the patient's affairs, which remain the responsibility of the Court of Protection, nor to consent to treatment on their behalf. The principal importance of the Act, so far as elderly people are concerned, is that for the first time it gives a legal means, backed by proper safeguards, to compel elderly people suffering from severe dementia to reside in a residential home or to admit helpers — for example a home help — to their own home. Many local authorities are reluctant to use these powers and many doctors are reluctant to consider dementia to be a mental illness.

Nevertheless the powers are there and it is important that they should be properly used when necessary. Otherwise dementia sufferers will continue to be deprived of their homes without any legal authority or refused care because they cannot make a valid application on their own behalf for a residential place.

The Enduring Powers of Attorney Act 1985[4]

This Act allows the donor of a Power of Attorney to sign a special form of Power called an Enduring Power of Attorney (EPA) which gives their attorney authority to continue to act even if the donor becomes mentally incapacitated. An ordinary Power, as is noted in Section 9, Protection of Attorney and third parties, lapses when the donor is no longer legally competent. An Enduring Power is not valid if the donor has already become incapable when he signs it. If the donor does become mentally incapable the attorney must apply to the Court of Protection to register the EPA and before doing this must notify the donor and the donor's closest relatives of the application.

If the opportunity afforded by this law is widely used it will lift a great deal of work from the Court of Protection and reduce the present widespread flouting of the law — whether deliberately or by ignorance. However some anxiety has been expressed that an EPA does give an unfettered discretion to the attorney which is wide open to abuse.

Disabled Persons (Services, Consultation and Representation) Act 1986[5]

This Act gives an enhanced right of assessment for local authority social services to all disabled people. It also, for the first time, gives legal recognition to the role of normal carers by requiring the local authority to take account of their needs when making the assessment. The actual phrasing of this section is worth quoting in full:

8. - (1) Where -

(a) a disabled person is living at home and receiving a substantial amount of care on a regular basis from another person (who is not a person employed to provide such care by any body in the exercise of its functions under any enactment), and

3

(b) it falls to a local authority to decide whether the disabled person's needs call for the provision by them of any services for him under any of the welfare enactments, the local authority shall, in deciding that question, have regard to the ability of that other person to continue to provide such care on a regular basis.

Also for the first time, the Act allows disabled people to appoint representatives to speak and receive information on their behalf, and requires local authorities to provide detailed reasons in writing for decisions made concerning service provision, with a duty to reconsider the matter further if asked to do so.

What the Act will mean in practice remains to be seen. It will be noted that local authorities are only required to explain their decision —there is still no right to any service, and the lack of enforcement of the minimal rights which are provided under the Chronically Sick and Disabled Persons Act 1970[6] does not bode well for its successor. Nevertheless it does give an important means of protection and appeal to disabled people and their representatives and carers, and it is essential that it should be used by disabled people of any age who are not satisfied with the level of service which they are receiving.

Other relevant publications

It is impossible to review the very wide range of work relating to this field which has been published since 1980, including many CPA Reports. However attention must be drawn to *The law and vulnerable elderly people*[7], which elaborates and updates information on many of the topics raised in *Rights and Risk*, and discusses the possible extension of the law to give elderly people a legal right to both services and protection. Another useful summary is *Services for elderly people*[8], published by the British Association of Social Workers, which provides an excellent statement of the principles of good social work in this field. For those who are concerned with the analysis of 'risk' as well as the definition of 'rights', Paul Brearley's introductory volume to a series on 'Hazards and helping', entitled *Risk and social work*[9], provides an illuminating and detailed discussion of the component factors in 'risk' and ways in which possible courses of action can be weighed up. Finally, it may be appropriate to draw attention to the author's most recent publication in this field — a short discussion paper entitled *Aspects of ageism*[10], which CPA has published as part of its 40th anniversary celebrations, and which draws attention to the great distance between the lip service paid to the rights and dignity of elderly people and the reality which they experience.

REFERENCES

1. *Registered Homes Act 1984,* Chapter 23. HMSO, London, 1984.
2. *Home life: a code of practice for residential care.* Centre for Policy on Ageing, London, 1984.
3. *Mental Health Act 1983,* Chapter 20: Statutes in force — official revised edition. HMSO, London, 1983.
4. *Enduring Powers of Attorney Act 1985,* Chapter 29. HMSO, London, 1985.
5. *Disabled Persons (Services, Consultation and Representation) Act 1986,* Chapter 33. HMSO, London, 1986.
6. *Chronically Sick and Disabled Persons Act 1970,* Chapter 44. HMSO, London, 1970.
7. *The law and vulnerable elderly people.* Age Concern England, Mitcham, 1986.
8. *Services for elderly people: a position statement,* prepared by the Services for Elderly People Project Group. British Association of Social Workers, Birmingham, 1982.
9. C. Paul Brearley, *Risk and Social Work.* Routledge and Kegan Paul, London, 1982.
10. A. Norman, *Aspects of ageism: a discussion paper.* Centre for Policy on Ageing, London, 1987.

Introduction

Liberty is an elusive concept. No human being has complete freedom of action. Ordinary people are constrained by work, income, housing, and a host of other factors which limit the range of courses open to them. For those who are frail or disabled and living on a pension, what they might like to do and what is physically or financially possible diverge still further. It would be unrealistic not to recognise that this is inevitable. However, there are ways in which society further restricts this narrowing range of choice by imposing on elderly people forms of care and treatment which are the fruit of social perception, social anxiety, convenience or custom rather than inescapable necessity. Old people are taken from their homes when domiciliary support and physical treatment might enable them to stay there; they are subjected in long-stay hospitals and homes to regimes which deprive them of many basic human dignities; and they are often not properly consulted about the care or treatment to which they are subjected.

This report attempts to examine how and why these things happen and what can be done to safeguard the liberty of elderly people. It is primarily concerned with those who are not only old but also severely disabled in mind or body, rather than with the problems of those who are physically and mentally fit but happen to have passed an arbitrarily-fixed 'pensionable age'. For that reason, it does not try to cover questions of compulsory and flexible retirement, important though these are. Also the report is based on *ad hoc* reading and enquiry rather than formal 'research' and it does not attempt to lay down rigid lines of right and wrong in this very complex area. It is presented by NCCOP as a discussion paper which is intended to raise issues and suggest lines of enquiry rather than to make definitive statements. The Corporation hopes to take further many of the issues which the report discusses.

It would be naïve to ignore the fact that disabled old people are competing with other members of society for finite resources, both voluntary and statutory, emotional and physical. 'Carers' also have rights and needs. The claims of children, younger disabled people, the mentally handicapped and the mentally ill have to be acknowledged. Yet if old people are to have genuine self-determination, they must be offered genuine alternatives. If, for example, standards of housing and levels of domiciliary support and treatment are not sufficient to make possible a reasonable level of warmth, cleanliness and nutrition, disabled old people have as little choice in whether or not to give up their homes as if they had been ordered away from them under Section 47 of the National Assistance Act. If nursing and care staff are so hard-pressed by shortage of personnel and the weight of very high levels of dependency that they have neither the time nor the energy to deal with those in their care as individuals, then they will be dealt with as 'bodies', regardless of training or official policy. However, although disabled elderly people are inevitably heavy service users, many of the suggestions made in this report do not call for a massive increase in resources. They do call for a much more skilled, varied and sensitive use of the resources which we already have, and above all for an underlying shift in *attitudes* towards the very old and disabled – away from a patronising and paternalistic over-protection from risk and towards acknowledgement of their right to as much self-determination as is possible for each individual within the limits of the resources available.

Society is not consistent in the risks it allows and those which it attempts to defend itself against. Some people are allowed to take risks and others are prevented from doing so. For example, mountain-climbing and pot-holing continue in spite of grumbles about the cost of rescue operations and an occasional fatal accident, yet paraplegics are often prevented from using public buildings because they cannot climb stairs and they might not be able to escape if there was a fire and the lift was immobilised. Their own wish to accept that risk is ignored.

Society also treats people in institutions differently from the way it treats invididuals. People in their own houses are not compelled to have even a fire-extinguisher at hand. Yet fire-officers impose crippling demands for fire precautions in old people's homes – demands which may force fees to be raised to a level which residents cannot meet, impose barriers to mobility and sometimes force homes to shut down or other services to be drastically cut back. The residents themselves are never asked what level of risk they themselves consider acceptable, and how they rate the danger of burning to death as compared with the danger of homelessness because they can no longer afford the fees, or the danger of immobilisation because they cannot get through a fire door when using a walking frame.

When one comes to questions of individual risk and protection the problems become more complex still. As Paul Brearley points out:

> The practitioner's life is not made any easier by the general nature of much of the legislation. The National Assistance Act, for instance, speaks of 'care and attention', the Health Services and Public Health Act of promoting the welfare of the elderly and the most recent memorandum on health services in old people's homes of 'support', 'care', and 'attention'. The extent and nature of social workers' duty to protect old people is unclear and their vulnerability to criticism is consequently heightened.[1]

The practitioner thus has to take into account potential damage to his own personal and professional reputation as well as possible danger to others and danger to the person who is perceived to be 'at risk'. We need much better analytical tools for assessing the hazards, dangers, and strengths of a particular situation so that the risks involved in action or inaction can be properly weighed up. Brearley has done some innovative work in this field and his analytical framework for the assessment of risk should become a basic tool in the training of both field and residential social workers.[2]

Problems of assessment become particularly difficult when the persons concerned are suffering from some degree of 'confusion' or 'dementia' and are therefore less able to have a realistic knowledge of their own situation and less able to convince others that their wishes should be respected. There is no doubt, as the work of Meacher and others has shown, that these people are most likely to have all decisions made for them, even when they retain considerable areas of mental awareness. This field of concern is dealt with in some detail in another NCCOP report and is therefore not discussed as a separate issue in this paper. (See publication list on p. 96). However, it must be recognised that the explosion in the numbers of the very old which is already occurring and will continue until after the end of the century, will almost certainly entail an explosion in the numbers of those suffering from some degree of chronic brain failure as well as from mental confusion caused by physical illness, adverse effects of drugs and/or the effect of bereavement, isolation and depression. It is therefore of great importance that the caring professions should make a particular effort to focus on ways in which the right to self determination of those suffering from some kind or degree of 'confusion' can best be protected.

The risks of choosing the 'safest' solution for mentally frail old people are vividly illustrated in an article by Dr A. A. Baker in which he describes a scene which, as he says, must be familiar to many doctors, social workers and members of the public:

> . . . an old lady lives alone, with a neglected garden and dilapidated house. She has gradually lost her contacts with the outside world, and the circle of friends and neighbours who had helped her with shopping and visits has diminished as she has become increasingly dirty and neglected. She has discouraged home help and meals on wheels services and is now living in squalor and is perhaps incontinent. Her memory is failing and general health becoming frail. She may already be known to the police because of wandering from the house, and neighbours and others have begun to put pressure on the medical and social services to have her removed. An incident such as a fall in the house, a fire, or another episode of wandering or fear of hypothermia has brought the firm request that she should be admitted to hospital.

Admission is arranged, sometimes by simple persuasion of a muddled old lady and sometimes by use of section 25 of the Mental Health Act, or other legal framework. Most of those concerned feel a sense of relief and say to themselves that she will be better off in hospital.

There, it is usually argued, she will be safer and have a longer life, a better quality of life, and better medical and nursing care. The facts, however, are not so comforting.

Baker goes on to say that in his psychiatric hospital it had been found that 25% of patients of this kind died within three weeks of admission, although some of them were physically healthy when admitted. The cause of death is usually a terminal broncho-pneumonia, and the pattern of events is often similar:

The patient is admitted, bathed, redressed, and within twenty-four hours may be hardly recognisable as the same person as the dirty tattered, old woman crouched at home by her fire. On the other hand, the old woman crouched by the fire often had a good deal to say for herself, showed both individuality and determination, and could be self-assertive. In hospital, however, the same old woman may appear bewildered, restless, look around in perplexity and seem unable to express any need other than, perhaps, the desire to get home. The initial restlessness, often with wandering round the ward and looking in vain for familiar places or people, will give way to apathy and dejection. This may happen spontaneously, but it may also be induced by medication. In the phase of apathy, appetite is often diminished, incontinence develops, and physical frailty with falls becomes more obvious. At some point, perhaps after a fall, or because the change in the patient's appearance causes concern, she is put to bed, within a day or two develops chest symptoms, and dies a day or two later.

Some, of course, survive the shock of hospital admission, but Baker questions whether those who are kept as long-term patients are really better off than if they had stayed at home. He describes the ward routine, alternating between meals and the lavatory, and the close symbiosis which develops between patients and nurses.

> . . . the patients are totally dependent on the nurses for survival and the nurses take obvious pleasure and pride in attending to the patients' basic needs, often addressing them by special names or endearments. The similarity between care for these totally dependent old women and the care required by a newborn baby is, of course, striking. Some patients seem to survive in a totally demented and dependent state for several years, thanks to the most excellent and devoted nursing care. Death however, cannot be evaded for ever, and the final months of many of these patients' lives can be very distressing.

Baker describes in detail the long-drawn-out and painful dying of one such old lady and concludes:

> There can be no doubt that the life of some of these elderly patients is considerably extended by nursing and medical care. There must be considerable doubt whether this extension is in any sense beneficial to the patient. Skilled nursing care can maintain life in a frail, elderly patient whose general condition is such that a comparable state in an animal might well lead to prosecution of the owner. Senile dementing processes sometimes lead to a relatively quick and peaceful death. Many, however, particularly under modern conditions of treatment, can be very cruel illnesses indeed. The problems of dying, particularly in patients with pain from tumours, have been discussed fairly widely recently, and there is a much better understanding of the process and of the medical and nursing approach that is needed. There is a similar need to discuss the problems of dying when there is no acute process and a prolonged terminal phase is likely. Cruelty to the elderly can take many forms. Co-operation between medical practitioner and social services should make it possible for the frail elderly to die in peace and dignity in their own homes, even if alone.[3]

This article has been quoted at length because it illustrates many of the questions with which this report is concerned. How far should old people be allowed to live in squalor if they refuse help? What level of danger or inconvenience to neighbours outweighs an individual's right to remain in his own home? What use should be made of compulsion under the Mental Health Act or the National Assistance Act? How does one balance the risks of institutionalisation against the risks of remaining independent? How can institutional care preserve the identity of those being cared for? How can the care of the dying be improved. How can the legal and social rights of mentally disabled old people be protected?

Inevitably, in trying to survey such issues, the report emphasises the failures in the system rather than the efforts which are constantly being made to improve the quality of caring. This effect is unavoidable, but the author wishes to pay tribute to the high level of awareness and concern about these questions which she invariably met with while preparing this report and to thank the many informants whose freely given knowledge and experience made the report possible.

REFERENCES

1. P. Brearley, 'Understanding risk', *Social Work Today*, Vol. 10, No. 31, April 3, 1979.
2. P. Brearley, *Social work a risky business* and other papers, available from the author, Department of Social Theory and Institutions, University College of North Wales, Bangor LL57 2DG.
3. A. A. Baker, 'Slow euthanasia or – "She will be better off in hospital"', *British Medical Journal*, 1976, No. 2, pp. 571–2.

Losing Your Home

It is not sufficiently realised that the loss of one's home – however good the reasons for leaving it – can be experienced as a form of bereavement and can produce the same grief reaction as the loss of a close relative. Peter Marris in his book *Loss and Change*[1] quotes a study of the reactions of families moved from the West End of Boston under an urban renewal scheme in which it was concluded that:

> for the majority it seems quite precise to speak of their reactions as expressions of *grief*. These are manifest in the feelings of painful loss, the continued longing, the general depressive tone, frequent symptoms of psychological or social or somatic distress, the active work required in adapting to the altered situation, the sense of helplessness, the occasional expressions of both direct and displaced anger, and the tendencies to idealise the lost place. At their most extreme, these reactions of grief are intense, deeply felt and, at times, overwhelming.

Altogether about half the 250 women and 316 men studied said they had been severely depressed or disturbed for a while, and another quarter had been more mildly upset. A quarter of the women were still very depressed two years after they had moved, while a fifth had taken over six months to recover their spirits. The unhappiest exiles described their loss in similar phrases to the bereaved: 'I felt as though I had lost everything'. 'It was like a piece being taken from me'. 'Something of me went with the West End'.

Similar reactions were described by Young and Wilmott when they studied families moved from the East End of London to a suburban housing estate and by Marris in a study of slum clearance in Lagos, where residents complained bitterly 'it seemed like being taken from happiness to misery', 'I fear it like death'. Marris suggests that, like bereavement, a change of home should be understood as a potential disruption of the meaning of life. Those for whom a move represents the realisation of a social status and way of life with which they already identify will be able to work through the loss and re-create what they valued in their former neighbourhood. 'But,' he says:

> for some, it may be a profound disturbance from which they never recover. And such tragedies are, I believe, more likely, the more slum clearance is used as an instrument of social change, not merely physical development; and the more it is directed against groups in society, whose non-conformity with the ruling values seems to stand in the way of progress.

Old people who are moved into sheltered housing or residential care may or may not be moved from slum conditions, but the sense of loss must surely be equally great for them. Indeed it may be greater if, in the process, they have to sacrifice not only a home and neighbourhood but the greater part of the possessions of a lifetime. It must also be true that they are likely to work through the loss only if they make a positive identification with their new life. If they are being moved in conformity with ruling social values which are offended by letting them stay where they are, or are forced to go by the physical duress of having no viable alternative, they are still less likely to recover from the loss.

A good deal of research data, much of it American, supports such a conclusion, and it is clear that the loss of a home may be particularly serious for those who are mentally impaired, physically ill, or depressed and thus unable to make a positive effort to identify with the new life. Gutman and Herbert[2] in 1976 quoted thirteen studies which showed that the death rate of elderly persons was unusually high during the first year after 'relocation' and particularly during the first three months. This was so regardless of whether the movement was from the community into a mental institution, from one institution to another, from one ward to another within the same institution, or from old to new facilities. (The same researchers showed from their own study however, that this effect does not obtain when the community moves *en bloc* to a new building with improved facilities and every effort is made to prepare patients and relatives for the move well in advance, to keep friends together in their new quarters and to transfer staff as well as patients.)

M. A. Lieberman, in an important paper on relocation and social policy described four studies which he had made: 'one on healthy moving into affluent high-care, sophisticated institutions; others involving sick, highly debilitated human beings moving into circumstances that would delight a muckraker'. These 'have yielded roughly comparable findings. Namely, no matter what the condition of the individual, the nature of the environment or the degree of sophisticated preparation, relocation entails a higher than acceptable risk to the large majority of those being moved.' Given that relocation may sometimes be inevitable, Lieberman goes on to ask what steps can be taken to minimise the risk but cannot suggest a solution. He concludes that careful preparation and 'working through' of the transitional process and impending loss, important though it may be relieving human misery, is not a powerful tool in minimising relocation risk. 'The reason,' he says, 'is not poor practice but rather incorrect strategy. Relocation is a risk to the individual not because of the symbolic meaning that such transitions imply, but because it entails radical changes in the life space of an individual that require new learning for adaptive purposes. Over and over again, studies on relocation report findings that physical status, cognitive ability and certain other characteristics of personality are powerful predictors to the outcome of relocation.' In other words, those who need institutional support the *least* are those who are most likely to survive the move into it, and 'it is often the very people who require supportive services that can be shown to entail the greatest risk.' (He adds that this is another illustration of how the results of empirical research often fail to help with the nitty-gritty of policy issues).[3]

A study of fatal home accidents made recently by the Tavistock

16

Institute of Human Relations on behalf of the Department of Prices and Consumer Protection also suggests that old people are not necessarily safer when they are 'in care'. The authors found that out of 133 fatal accidents studied in the '65 and over' age group (75% caused by falls) 35% were in institutional care, although only 4·8% of this age group live in institutions. They comment 'Even considering that residential institutions contain a higher proportion of the infirm, the difference in accidental deaths is high'.[4]

It would seem to follow from all this, that if avoidance of 'risk' is indeed a prime objective, moving people out of their homes may not be the best way of achieving it, and that the more they appear to be at risk where they are, the worse will be their prognosis if they are moved. Yet this is a factor which is so seldom taken into consideration when considering transfer into residential care, and still less is it taken into consideration when deciding on hospital admission.

Elderly people, like members of any other age group, are of course often admitted to hospital for surgery or investigation which could not be provided in their own home; and they may benefit greatly from such treatment. (For example, a study of 248 patients over 80 admitted as emergencies to acute surgical wards of the Reading hospitals in 1976 showed that the overall mortality rate was 21·8% and it fell to 12·5% if terminal disease was excluded. All but seven patients were discharged home.)[5] However, there is another large group of elderly people who become patients not so much because their condition demands full-scale hospital treatment as because there is a crisis in their system of social support. The social crisis then has a medical label attached to it in order to make the admission acceptable to the hospital. For example, if an elderly person develops pneumonia and the spouse finds the anxiety of nursing at home too much to bear, an admission will probably be arranged, but the diagnosis is pneumonia, not 'anxiety in spouse'. Very often the admission may be occasioned by some incident or accident which proves to be the last straw on an already over-strained support system, or because there is no time to arrange for the domiciliary services required by a change in circumstances (such as the caring relative becoming sick). Or, if an elderly person presents at an Accident and Emergency department of a hospital after, say, a fall in the street, a harassed houseman may 'play safe' and keep the person in for 'investigation' just to make sure no damage has been done.

The problem is that it is much easier for an elderly person to become a hospital patient than to cease to be one. There are a number of reasons for this. The 'social space' in which the person has been living may close behind him on admission, so that he cannot get back. A family may heave a sigh of relief, having realised, perhaps for the first time, what a burden it has been carrying and say 'he's not coming back here'. A landlord may take the opportunity to re-possess his house, or the warden of a sheltered housing complex say 'He needs too much nursing now, I can't cope'. Ironically, it is often the person who would appear to be most at risk, who lives alone in his own home, who is in least danger of having his social space close up on him.

It is also often the case that if a person has only just been coping with independent life, hospital admission breaks a tenuous level of confidence which can only be restored with time, care and skill. Elderly people who are suffering from some degree of dementia are especially at risk because the experience of admission to a totally strange and unfamiliar environment is likely to increase confusion and generate problems such as falling and incontinence which may not have been present before.

Another possibility is that hospital 'investigation' may show up undiagnosed diseases which a person has been living with for years, but which, once diagnosed, the hospital may feel compelled to treat. Observation after a fall may then become treatment for something quite different, so that the person is confirmed in his patient status. Moreover, if the person is being treated in an acute ward, the nursing staff may not have the time, interest or training to help the patient to retain independence and mobility, and even a few days of inactivity may produce disuse atrophy which involves not only loss of muscle power but also loss of the range of movement normally possessed by a joint. Simple skills required for daily living such as combing one's hair, fastening a button or rising from a chair may then be lost. (It has been shown that even the muscle disuse occurring during normal sleep leads to significant weakness on waking).[6] A period of treatment in an acute ward may therefore mean that an elderly person requires a prolonged period of rehabilitation in a geriatric ward before he can recover his skills sufficiently to manage at home again – and the longer the period in hospital, the more likely it is that the 'social space' at home will have closed up.

For all these reasons, hospital admission – which can undoubtedly be 'life-saving' – may also be dangerous to elderly people, and the dangers need to be weighed against the advantages when deciding whether or not to admit someone to hospital.

Many of the comments made above about the way in which elderly people become patients apply with equal force to the way in which they become residents in old people's homes. Indeed, in some ways the process appears often to be an even more arbitrary response to social fears and pressures, or the failure of social support, rather than to be a carefully thought-out assessment of alternatives. This is all the more serious because the hospital patient is only *in danger* of becoming 'long-stay', but the resident in a home is virtually *certain* to be so. Once admitted on a permanent basis, there is little hope of returning to independence.

A recent research project in Coventry studied discrepancies between declared policy on admission to residential care and actual practice.[7] It was found that the social and medical information supplied to the allocation panel varied greatly in range and quality and that it did not include any information on take-up of domiciliary services, the physical nature of the applicant's dwelling, or the social composition of his household. Furthermore, the panel was required to fulfil two aims which were not necessarily compatible. It tried to ensure that all available places were utilised to their full extent and it tried to allocate places to those who were most in need. Since the number of places available varied week by week, an applicant might succeed in one week when he would have been turned down in another. The result was that it became pointless for the panel members to try to assess whether applicants met certain publicly known and objective criteria with the result that those putting applications forward had no means of knowing exactly what evidence should be provided. 'In consequence', the report says, 'there is a tendency on the part of those supporting an application to advocate the applicant's cause stressing a partisan view, and objective information is neglected.' The report concludes that the admission procedure did not succeed in the stated policy either of providing care for those whose level of dependency could no longer be met by the provision of all suitable domiciliary services, or in providing care for those who were most at risk. On the mitigation of risk, the writers found no difference between those who were admitted and those who were refused in respect of illness, disability, mental confusion, household setting or change in the level of risk. In practice, priority was given to those who lived alone, who were isolated from friends and neighbours and had themselves applied for admission. Priority was also given to those living with relatives who were no longer willing to care for them. (This situation often arose from the operation of family dynamics rather than any change in the level of the elderly person's dependency.) The writers believed that skilled social work combined with domiciliary support for the families concerned might sometimes have alleviated this problem and avoided the need for admission. In all cases they thought there should be 'consistent comprehensive information on the take up of domiciliary services' when applications are considered. At present there is no evidence that people move from a stage of increasing domiciliary support to residential care.

Other recent research also indicates that those admitted to residential care are not necessarily those who are most in need of it. For example, a study of 55 residents in homes in a rural area of Wales found that twelve of them had no regular outside help with domestic tasks before admission and 43% were only slightly or not at all incapacitated (using the Townsend scale). They were in fact somewhat less handicapped than the sample of old people living in the community and seeking help from a local authority department which were studied by E. M. Goldberg.[8] Similarly, a 1977 survey made in Northern Ireland found that 34% of the residents of all statutory homes could be classified as 'fit' and suggests that 'given increased numbers of old people's dwellings and additional sheltered housing, coupled with imaginative use of the whole range of supporting services, up to 826 men and women might have managed in their own homes for a further period at least.'[9] More detailed data is supplied by the preliminary findings of a study of 170 applicants for residential care in

Newham. 28% of the applicants had no inside lavatory and 30% had no bathroom; one third were not in receipt of any kind of domiciliary service at the time of referral, or had not been receiving such a service before admission to hospital. It does seem probable that with better housing conditions and more support at least some of these people need not have applied for admission to a home.[10]

Another fault in the usual procedure for deciding that admission to residential care is necessary is that there is seldom a medical assessment to check whether the mental or physical condition which is causing concern can be remedied. For example, whether confusion might be caused by 'drug cocktails', or self-neglect by depression. When, as an experiment, 100 old people in Manchester were medically screened at the time of their acceptance for residential care it was found that another form of care was more appropriate in 32 cases – hospital admission in 16, sheltered housing in 4, and remaining at home in 12. In only 20% of the cases were there no new findings although many of the patients were already receiving hospital or GP treatment. The screening facility was freely available on request yet those referred represented only 20% of the elderly people admitted to homes in the area during the period of study. The writer comments that 'they seem to have been selected by social workers particularly because of their apparent unfitness'. If this is true, it seems likely that the remaining 80% were even more likely to benefit from expert medical assessment and might thereby have been enabled to remain at home. Why was this facility not used? One suggestion (not made in the article) is that social workers see admission to residential care as their 'territory' and are reluctant to allow geriatricians the power of endorsing or failing to endorse their recommendations. Whatever the reason, there would seem to be a strong case, as the article suggests, for making a proper medical assessment a routine part of all admission procedures.[11]

Medical assessment may be inadequate for those moving from their own homes into residential care but there is also uncertainty about the adequacy of social assessment when people are discharged from hospital into a home. This is a very common route into residential care (over 50% of the applicants in the Newham study) and it seems likely that at least some of these cases arise because hospital staff are too anxious to allow the patient to try out their independence at home and (perhaps partly because of staff anxiety) the patient has lost confidence in his own ability to cope. Further, as has been noted, admission to hospital may cause a patient's social space to close behind him, so that although he may be fit to go home, the family will not allow it, or the landlord has repossessed the house or the sheltered flat has been re-let. In these circumstances, homes may resist admitting ex-hospital patients who really are dependent and need residential care because they are considered to be 'nursing' cases, while accepting those who, given sufficient and proper accommodation could perhaps manage in the community.

If assessment procedures are inadequate for the very serious step of taking someone from his own home for the rest of his life, the way in which application is discussed with the potential resident, and the actual admission procedure, may also leave a great deal to be desired. The Welsh study found that 19 (35% of their sample of 55) said that they had not wanted to become a resident (almost all these were people referred by officials or by relatives) and only 14 felt completely happy with the prospect, the remainder suffering 'greater or less unhappiness in contemplating the future'. Yet the social workers concerned were not felt by the respondents to have given any very clear idea of the practical consequences of entering a home, what the life there would be like, or what alternatives there might be. 'There was a feeling from their replies that the issue of whether or not they were to be admitted is already determined by the time of this interview' and that when life in residential care was discussed it was as an aid to persuasion. 'Talked about how nice the Home was', or 'You would be better off in a Home' were typical recollections. People were sometimes left with the impression that they could change to another home if they wished, or that they could return to their own home later, when this was not true. Only five of the 55 had visited the home to which they were admitted (and some of these had done so because of other contacts, not because of their own impending admission). Only one had been visited by a staff member. When a vacancy became available, a very short period was sometimes given to make a decision and move in, and the prospective residents were often informed indirectly of the vacancy (via relatives or hospital staff) so that there was no opportunity at that stage to discuss their final decision to accept or refuse the place. Ten of the sample were left to enter the Home unaccompanied by anyone – regardless that it was likely to be one of the most traumatic moments of their lives.

Nothing has yet been said about the part which relatives may play in the process of losing independence. This would seem to be a crucial area about which too little is known. It is, of course, very common, and socially approved, for a married son or daughter to invite an elderly parent to give up his own home and live with them, and if there is sufficient space, and sufficient physical and financial resources for the family to cope, this may work out very well. However, there are a number of inherent dangers in this course which may not be fully appreciated: first, the old person is still losing his *own* home, even if he is not going to an institution and the sense of psychological loss and need for personal adaptation can be as severe as if he was going into institutional care. This is especially true if the neighbourhood is different so that the contacts and customs of a life time are also lost. Second, it can never be certain that the family will be able or willing to continue to cope and in that case, the old person, having lost his own home, has no alternative to institutional care since it is likely to be almost impossible to set himself up again in independence. (The possible use of sheltered housing for situations of this kind needs to be explored.) Third, it is almost impossible for the caring relative to resist taking over from the old person, both physically and mentally – what might be called the 'I'll do it for you' syndrome. Traditional role playing has an interesting effect on this tendency. A study of elderly people living with single adult children has shown that severely disabled mothers living with sons will continue to cook and look after the house when less disabled mothers living with single daughters relinquish almost all household activity.[12]

It would seem that there is a need for much more public education about the advantages and disadvantages of taking an old person into one's home and about the danger of meeting the *relative's* anxieties and guilt feelings by this means, rather than looking objectively at what the old person himself really wants and needs.

The same is true of situations where relatives try to persuade an old person to go into a home, or put pressure on the local authority, or GP to arrange this. As was noted above, the Welsh study indicated that when the application is made by relatives, the old person is not likely to welcome the idea and if they do agree it tends to be 'because I don't want to be a burden'. Often the relatives may take this action because they are afraid that they will incur criticism if an accident occurs and the old person is living alone, but this guilt can be assuaged if a social worker or doctor suggests to them that the old person has a right to live as he likes and that if he wants to take risks it is up to him. One experienced social worker told the writer that elderly people themselves do not need social work – but their relatives do.

It seems clear that we should be working towards the achievement of a system in which people never give up their homes unless *either* they themselves genuinely wish to do so *or* it is physically impossible for them or their relatives to cope, using a full range of statutory and voluntary domiciliary services. In reaching one or other of these conclusions full account should be taken of reversible physical cause for inability to cope; feasible alterations in housing conditions; feasible provision of aids and adaptations; and the possible physical and psychological effects of moving into institutional care. When movement into residential care *is* decided on, the step should be prepared for and taken with the seriousness its importance deserves. A chart setting out 'good practice' in this field is attached as an appendix to this chapter.

The practice of admissions

Phase	Duration	Focus of work	Elements	Activities	Implications
I Preparation	From the time that an application for residential care is made up to the notification that a place is available.	Assessment and preparation of the prospective resident for life in residential care.	1 The application	Assessing the background to the application and the prospective resident. Exchanging basic information about the likely cost of residential care, its location and lifestyle.	A wide ranging assessment that includes home, social and psychological factors places the application in the context whereby the full needs rather than just the presenting ones can be evaluated. It will provide the basis for accepting or rejecting the application and developing the guidelines for ongoing work in community and/or residential care.
			2 Its outcome	Personal notification to the prospective resident of the outcome.	Acceptance of the application implies a level of need that justifies ongoing work in the interim period. In other cases preventive work may be appropriate.
			3 The choice of home	Giving prospective residents sufficient information upon which they may base 'choice' and anticipate meaningfully the life in an old people's home.	The opportunity should be provided for prospective residents to visit homes for single days and weekends. Preparation for changes in lifestyle begins.

Phase	Duration	Focus of work	Elements	Activities	Implications
II **Separation**	From the notification that a place is available to the moment of admission.	Achieving a smooth transition from community to residential life.	1 Notification	Informing the prospective resident personally of the home in which they are invited to live, its address, facilities, *etc*.	Information about the personal belongings, clothes, *etc*, that will be needed/can be taken to the home is passed on. Consultation about the remaining property, pets, *etc*, is begun.
			2 Confirmation	Confirmation of the initial application and deciding upon a mutually convenient date for admission.	Sufficient time should be allowed to complete admission arrangements satisfactorily.
			3 Separation	Saying farewell to neighbours, friends, *etc*, ensuring that at the same time they know of the new address.	Consider working with families of newly admitted residents to ensure visiting. Encourage the maintenance of links with the community.
			4 Transportation	Deciding with relatives, *etc*, the transfer arrangements, allowing sufficient time for it to be unhurried, sufficient space for personal belongings to be taken.	The continuity of contact between the social worker and the prospective resident should be maintained from the assessments and notification phases through to residential life itself.

Phase	Duration	Focus of work	Elements	Activities	Implications
III Transition	The first day in the new home.	Ensuring that the impact of the change in life between the community and residential home is managed sympathetically.	First meetings with: 1 Officer in charge 2 Staff 3 Residents 4 Routines 5 Physical environment	Arranging the most appropriate time to arrive at the home and creating an atmosphere where the introductions can be made most naturally. Ensuring that the new resident knows her way around the home and to whom to turn for advice, support and understanding,	Field and residential staff need to work together to co-ordinate their roles during the admission. Existing residents/staff in the home who may already know resident or her home area could be introduced to her. Choice of 'key worker' in the home.
IV Incorporation	From the end of the first day until the new resident looks on the home as 'home'.	Development of the residents' interests and life in the new home and in the community.	1 Development of new 'anticipations'	Formulation of a programme for residential care.	Working with the new resident to understand the impact of the change in life. Identifying the areas of stress and of development.
			2 Retaining existing social links and developing others.	Ensuring that the resident enjoys as full and as satisfying a life as can be provided.	Working with others in the community, the home and the social services department as a whole to meet the interests of residents.

Source: P. Pope, 'Admission to Residential Homes for the Elderly', *Social Work Today* Vol. 9 No. 44 July 18 1978

REFERENCES

1. P. Marris, *Loss and change*, Institute of Community Studies, Routledge & Kegan Paul, 1974.
2. G. M. Gutman & C. P. Herbert, 'Mortality rates among relocated extended care patients', *Journal of Gerontology 1976*, Vol. 31, No.3,352–357.
3. M. A. Lieberman, 'Symposium – Long-term care: Research, Policy & Practice'. *The Gerontologist*, Vol. 14, No. 6, December 1974.
4. B. Poyner and N. Hughes, *A classification of fatal home accidents*, The Tavistock Institute of Human Relations 2T140, 1978. (Report to the Department of Prices and Consumer Protection.)
5. R. Salem et al. 'Emergency geriatric surgical admission', *British Medical Journal 1978*, 2,416–417.
6. Bob Browne, 'Inactivity in the elderly', *Health and Social Service Journal*, Vol. 88, No. 4575, January 10, 1978 (quoting Wright V. et al. 'Joint Stiffness, its characterisation and significance'. *Biomed. Engin.* 4, i, 1969).
7. K. Carter and T. N. Evans, 'Intentions and achievements in admission of the elderly', in *Clearing House for Local Authority Social Services Research*, No. 9, 1978, pp. 71–99.
8. I. Shaw and R. Walton, 'Transitions to residence in homes for elderly' in *Rights to Residence*, edited by D. Harris and J. Hyland, Residential Care Association, 1979.
9. *The Need for Care – A census of residents in homes for the elderly*, Department of Health and Social Security, Social Work Advisory Group, Belfast, 1977.
10. B. Stapleton and R. Lee, *Survey of applicants for people's homes in Newham*, London Borough of Newham Social Services Department, 1979 (preliminary findings).
11. J. C. Brocklehurst et al. 'Medical screening of old people accepted for residential care', *The Lancet*, No. 8081, July 15, 1978.
12. F. Wright, *Care of elderly disabled parents in the community by single sons and daughters*, Social Research Unit, Bedford College (preliminary findings).

Compulsory Care

The previous chapter described various informal channels by which elderly people may find themselves in institutional care without themselves feeling any strong need or wish for it. This section describes how such a move can be legally forced on elderly people through the operation of Section 47 of the National Assistance Act 1948, and its 1951 Amendment.

The relevant section of the 1948 Act states.

47. (1) The following provisions of this section shall have effect for the purposes of securing the necessary care and attention for persons who –
(a) are suffering from grave chronic disease or, being aged, infirm or physically incapacitated, are living in insanitary conditions, and
(b) are unable to devote to themselves, and are not receiving from other persons, proper care and attention.

(2) If the medical officer of health certifies in writing to the appropriate authority that he is satisfied after thorough enquiry and consideration that in the interests of any such person as aforesaid residing in the area of the authority, or for preventing injury to the health of, or serious nuisance to, other persons, it is necessary to remove any such preson as aforesaid from the premises in whch he is residing, the appropriate authority may apply to a court of summary jurisdiction having jurisdiction in the place where the premises are situated for an order under the next following subsection.

The magistrate, if 'satisfied on oral evidence of the allegations in the certificate, and that it is expedient to do so' can then order the removal of the person concerned to a 'suitable hospital or other place' for a period of up to three months, and the order can thereafter be renewed indefinitely. However, this Section 47 does require seven days' notice to be given to the person concerned so that he or she can appeal. The 1951 Amendment allows removal without any delay for a period of three weeks if two doctors (one being the Medical Officer of Health) state that in their opinion this is necessary. This Order can be made by any Justice of the Peace who has jurisdiction in the area concerned, not only by a Court in session, but it must be renewed by a Court after three weeks if it is to remain valid. It is this version of the Act which is now most frequently used.

Given the emphasis which English law usually lays upon the right to personal liberty, the history of this Section 47 makes surprising reading. Dr Muir Gray, who has done some research on the matter, describes its origins as follows:

> The obvious avenue to explore initially was that of Poor Law legislation. The Webbs believed that such a power should be introduced, stating in the Minority Report of the Poor Law Commission which they edited and largely wrote, that 'There is no subject brought before us on which there has been such unanimity of testimony as the need, in the public interests, for some power of compulsory removal of infirm old men or women who refuse to accept an order for admission to the Workhouse, and who linger on, alone and uncared for, in the most shocking conditions of filth and insanitation.' (Source: Page 352, The Minority Report of the Poor Law Commission, Vol. 1: The Break up of the Poor Law. Edited and introduced by S. & B. Webb. Longman Green & Co., 1909.)
>
> The Webbs appeared to view such an innovation not as an extension of the Poor Law – in fact, they were opposed to such powers being given to the 'Destitution Authority' – but as a logical extension of the powers vested in the various public health acts which had been

drafted to allow Local Health Authorities to prevent the spread of infectious disease. That was in 1909. The next reference to this principle which I have found so far in my research is in Section 56 of the Bradford Corporation Act of 1925. The Parliamentary Select Committee which considered this local bill reported that 'the proposal introduced an entirely new principle, and that it was approved by them after hearing evidence and upon very careful consideration'. The Section found its way into the London County Council (General Powers) Act 1928, with little modification, partly to help individuals in need but also, it appears, to facilitate their slum clearance programme. Section 28 was transposed to become Section 224 of the Public Health (London) Act 1936 and thence, again almost verbatim, to Section 47 of the National Assistance Act 1948.[1]

The power then, appears to derive not so much from a wish to protect the elderly person at risk, as from the need to facilitate slum clearance or prevent infection. The history of the Section is related to housing and environmental health rather than to welfare considerations, though of course the Section's history does not necessarily influence its present use.

When Aneurin Bevan introduced the Second Reading of the National Assistance Bill, Section 47 (then Section 46) was challenged by a Conservative, Lieutenant-Colonel Elliott, on the basis that one medical certificate was an inadequate basis on which to deprive someone of their liberty. Bevan said, 'It comes to Court'. 'Yes,' said Elliott, 'but it makes no provision at all for the person being examined by the Court or summoned. The only person who has to conduct an examination is the certifying officer'. 'He is the Medical Officer of Health', Bevan replied. 'True', said Elliot, 'but two certificates are usually necessary before taking the pretty grave step of removing a citizen from his house and detaining him under an indeterminate sentence on an indeterminate order.' Bevan then asked if Elliott would agree that when an old person is utterly incapable of looking after himself and in a very bad state of health and insanitary condition some authority must be responsible for looking after them and someone must do something about it? 'It is in the interests of old people themselves that this power is taken and not in the interests of a tyrannical State.' Elliott answered by saying that 'no one will quarrel with extreme cases, but what about borderline ones?' 'Should the Court decide on the evidence of one man?' Another MP then suggested that this was an imputation on the medical profession!

This discussion covered about one page of Hansard and was the only reference to the Section in the 133 pages covering the debate – apart from a few sour general references to Colonel Elliott's speech (one member called it 'the worst carping speech I have ever heard'.) The Section was only slightly altered in committee and was not questioned in any way during the Third Reading.

There can be no better indication of the very low status which the disadvantaged elderly occupy in society than this very cursory treatment of their fundamental liberty.

The 1951 Amendment, which removed any possibility of effective resistance to removal by giving no time to appeal before the event, received still shorter shrift. It was a Private Member's Bill presented by a Dr Broughton, who told the House how a spinster, aged 52, and described by a relative as being 'eccentric and stubborn' had fallen in the street and broken her thigh bone. 'She was helped home by a neighbour and she then refused all further assistance. She lay on the floor and would not accept the services of doctor, nurse or home help. The Medical Officer of Health was called and advised her removal to hospital but she refused this also and so he took action under Section 47. However this could not be effected without seven days' notice (in practice nine days) and by that time the woman had contracted tetanus and died soon after her removal to hospital. He asked the House to allow emergency action to be taken on the recommendation of two doctors. The Bill had general support and was passed without more ado – in all the discussion covered one page of Hansard.

Dr Muir Gray describes what happened to the Act's administration after 1974 as follows:

In the re-organisation of local government the power to operate Section 47 passed to district councils, a different tier of authority from social service departments in non-metropolitan areas. The officer responsible, previously the Medical Officer of Health, became the Community Physician, who was nominated as 'Proper Officer' to the district council. In health authorities which do not have health districts – called single district health authorities – the Medical Officer for Environmental Health (sometimes called the Specialist in Community Medicine for Environmental Health) is the Proper Officer to all the district councils in the area. He acts as the Medical Officer of Health used to and may delegate his power in this and other areas of environmental health, such as infectious disease control and housing, to other Community Physicians. In health authorities which are divided into a number of health districts, as most are, the District Community Physician is the Proper Officer.

The consequence is that in some Shire Counties, the Proper Officer may have an excellent knowledge of epidemic control or sanitation problems but have very little contact with social services or domiciliary health services, no experience in communicating with elderly people and no control over the resources needed to care for someone in their own home. Even in the Metropolitan Districts, the Proper Officer may be (as in Birmingham) the Environmental Health Specialist. And even if the Community Physician concerned is knowledgeable and informed, it does not follow that when he is off duty his substitutes will be equally experienced.

It is a further indication of how lightly elderly people's civil rights are regarded, that no national statistics are kept concerning the use of Section 47. Before 1974 Medical Officers were at least required to record Section 47 removals in their Annual Report. Now even this has lapsed and in some cases authorities may even have difficulty in producing their own figures because when several community physicians have authority to act, they do not always pool their records. However, it appears from the preliminary results of a survey of Proper Officers, recently carried out by Dr Muir Gray, that the Section is still used as frequently as it was before 1974 – an average of about 200 cases a year. *Ad hoc* enquiry indicates that some authorities – Liverpool and Birmingham for example – use the section about twelve to fifteen times a year. Others, which have very similar social conditions, have Proper Officers who are opposed to the use of the Act in principle and never use it at all. Those who take this line say that with proper domiciliary and health services, and sufficient time and care given to building up a relationship, forcible removal is not needed. Insanitary conditions can be cleaned up and kept clean by a special squad of home helps; terminal nursing care can be provided, and when a relationship of trust has been established, the person can often be persuaded to accept treatment. Alternatively, the Public Health Act 1936 may be used to force acceptance of domiciliary services on a client if the squalor in which they are living is becoming a public nuisance.

There is equally great variety of opinion concerning what the Section actually means and the circumstances in which it can properly be used, not surprisingly, since it contains no definitions, and no guidelines for its use have been issued.

The relevant form requires the doctors concerned to state that the person is *either* suffering from grave chronic disease *or* being aged, infirm or physically incapacitated, is living in insanitary conditions *and* is unable to devote to himself and is not receiving from other persons, proper care and attention.

One community physician takes the view that this precludes him from making an order on someone who is reasonably physically fit, however insanitary the living conditions may be, and also that he cannot make an order on someone who is suffering from an *acute* illness such as pneumonia (even though the reason given in Parliament for the 1951 Amendment indicates that the Act was expected to be used to compel treatment for accidental injury). At the other extreme, a community physician in Liverpool believes that it is most justifiable to use the Section when medical treatment has some hope of doing positive good or saving life and has had no hesitation in using it when a person was thought to be a serious fire hazard, even though physically fit. Another believes 'that if we moved everyone who was a fire

34

hazard we would have to move half the population' and thinks that the Act should only be used if there is a really serious public danger, not merely some degree of risk or inconvenience to neighbours from wandering in the street, leaving on gas taps, or living in insanitary conditions.

Attitudes also differ about whether or not the Section should be used when a person appears to be dying and wishes to die in his own home. Some believe that if the disease is not infectious (such as TB) the wishes of the sick person should be respected; others point out that in practice it can be very difficult to withstand pressure from the GP, who himself may be pressurised by home helps, neighbours, etc., especially as the community physician is not himself in a position to provide medical and nursing care and cannot force others to do so. Also, without proper examination and tests it may be very difficult to tell whether the person actually is terminally ill. Another factor is fear of adverse newspaper comment or comment from the coroner if the person dies alone and uncared for and there may be panic action on Friday evening if it is feared that the person will die at the weekend when services are minimal[2] (see p. 77).

Options also differ as to whether the Section should be used to admit people to hospital or to residential care. In Darlington, for example, it has only been used to compel removal to hospital on the ground that a proper medical check is essential before any further action is taken. In Birmingham, on the other hand, 12 out of 15 cases in 1978 went straight into residential care and some doctors take the view that it should *only* be used for admission to residential care because medical treatment without consent is assault (see p. 65).

The responsibilities of the magistrate under the Section are equally unclear. In some areas, magistrates always visit the person concerned (presumably on the advice of their Clerk); in other places they simply sign the form presented to them, and elsewhere again it is left to their own initiative which course to follow. However, it seems clear that whichever they do, their official role is to see that the case comes within the legal definitions required and not in any way to represent the patient's interests. It does not appear that they are given any advice or instruction about their responsibility under the Act, and casual enquiry indicates that some do not even know they have this power, let alone have views on how it should be exercised.

These very wide variations in practice and interpretation would seem to indicate a serious cause for concern. As Dr S. S. Bakhshi, one of the community physicians for Birmingham, put it:

> The way in which the Act is used and attitudes to it have developed over time in each local authority. It is a poor relation and usually left entirely to the responsible officer in interpreting it. No one really bothers how and why the Act is administered.

There is a case for abolishing this Section of the Act altogether. If some areas find that time, patience and good social work make it unnecessary to use it, why not all? Others would argue that in these areas illegal strong-arm methods must sometimes be used and that the Act does at least provide a legal safeguard and proper procedure which leaves the person concerned with the dignity of having his wishes acknowledged and formally refused rather than implying that he is mentally incapable by using compulsion under the Mental Health Act, or slipping him a sedative, or simply telling him that he has no alternative but to comply. Whatever the merits of these arguments, it does seem clear that there is a need for proper investigation of the way in which Section 47 is used and authoritative comment on how it should be interpreted and administered. This should be accompanied by enquiry as to whether the powers which it confers still need to be retained, and if so whether the legal procedure should be revised. Such action will be of little use, however, unless greater attention is paid to the training and preparation of community physicians in the performance of their duties under the Act. No one would claim that they use the Section lightly at present. Forcible removal is a traumatic occasion for everyone involved and it demands painful decisions about freedom and risk. Also the scarcity of longstay facilities does not encourage casual use of the Act. Nevertheless, the present wide variations in its use and interpretation, and the complexity of the issues involved, do indicate that the Faculty of Community Medicine of the Royal College of Physicians should be giving this issue more attention than it now receives. At present the Faculty has no policy on the training of community physicians who act as Proper Officers under the Act and the issue has not been mentioned in two recent reports on the work of the community physicians and community health doctors.[3]

NCCOP would welcome views concerning the operation of the Section and accounts of any experience relating to its use.

REFERENCES

1. M. Gray, 'Forcing old people to leave their homes', *Community Care*, March 8, 1979.
2. S. G. Rubin and A. J. R. Scott-Samuel, 'When community care fails', *Health and Social Service Journal*, January 10, 1976.
3. *Report of the working party on the state of community medicine*, Chairman Dr G. Duncan, and *Report of the working party on community health doctors*, Chairman Dr J. P. Preston, both obtainable from the British Medical Association, BMA House, Tavistock Square, WC1

Freedom in Residential Care

When elderly people do enter long-term residential care, what liberty of choice and action do they have a 'right' to enjoy and what must they expect to surrender as the price of security and care?

The concept of 'rights' is complex and no two writers are likely to agree on a definition – as is evident in a collection of papers published by the Residential Care Association, the foreword of which says:

> Despite the development of a rights industry over the past decade, any rights we might claim only exist insofar as they are granted by those around us. In a very real way, a right is nothing more or less than statement of the relationship between individual and community, or between individual and individual. Clearly this relationship is now sophisticated and institutionalised in many areas of our lives, particularly those relating to aspects of welfare provision in the widest sense. The relationship is essentially and correctly a fluid one, which is subject to influence, argument and change – evolved or imposed. The frustration of considering any form of rights is that there are few absolute and timeless rights, and the concept of a right cannot be divorced from the concept of responsibility and of need.
>
> In looking at the rights of people in residential and day care it would be tempting to assume that there are absolute and timeless rights that can, or should be, applicable to every recipient of that care. In reality these

rights are affected by the person's own needs; the needs of other residents; the needs and competence of staff members; and the wider societal framework.[1]

Nevertheless, without becoming too philosophic about definitions, it can probably be accepted that elderly people in care should enjoy the liberty granted to any other adult citizen to order his activities, finances and personal affairs, subject only to restrictions which are necessary in order to provide the level of care he needs, or to protect the quality of life of other residents and of the care givers.

How far can residential homes be said to live up to such a goal? Undoubtedly, in the more enlightened local authorities and in a good proportion of the voluntary and private homes, there has been a great deal of improvement over the last few years. Real though sporadic efforts are being made to encourage normal active living in as homelike conditions as possible, even if this involves some degree of risk. Nevertheless, a great deal remains to be done. A recent DHSS study of 124 local authority, voluntary and private homes in the London area found that only 18% could be described as 'providing a home, in the true sense, for their residents', and at the other end of the scale, 15% were categorised as 'institutional' and described as 'rigid', 'unrelaxed' and 'tense'. In very few of the homes was there any form of consultation with the residents about the way life was organised; most of them did not encourage residents to help with chores or do things for themselves; few had any written or published statements of tasks or objectives. In about one-third of the homes early morning tea was served at 6.00 a.m. and in some residents were called even earlier. The last main meal was usually served before 5.00 p.m. and some homes required residents to be in bed by 7.30 p.m. Lack of privacy, compulsory surrender of pension books and the absence of opportunity to make choices and decisions were also commented upon in the report.[2] The London Boroughs are certainly not exceptional in this respect and it seems likely from NCCOP's own experience in operating its Homes Advice service that the same problems, and the same very wide variations in quality of life, can be found all over the country.

As the Residential Care Association said in its comments on the DHSS Discussion Document *A happier old age*:

> An enormous amount of work still needs to be done in improving the amount of personal freedom open to residents in residential accommodation. Some of the better Homes are attempting to maintain human dignity and preserve freedom wherever possible, but far too often the attitude remains that when people come into care they become subject to the system and needs of the staff which involves a massive loss of personal dignity and individual freedom. Examples are lack of choice of menu, the inability to come and go outside the Home, staff present at bathing time, set meal times, etc.
>
> We believe that residents should be able to keep their own pension books, choose the type of food they eat, to come and go in the residential establishment as they please, get up and go to bed at times which suit themselves, have meal times over a flexible period, choose their own clothes, have access to meal and snack facilities, please themselves if and when they have a bath subject to the need to bath relatively frequently, have access to private facilities where they can receive relatives and friends and also be actively encouraged to take a hand in the running of the Home. We appreciate that for some residents a free life involves some amount of risk, but risk is part of normal life and it must be accepted by both Social Services Departments, members and residential staff that independent living should be encouraged even though there are elements of risk.

Similar points are made in more detail in the Personal Social Services Council report *Residential care reviewed* and in numerous other publications.

Why then, is improvement so slow and so uneven? Any number of reasons can be put forward: the increasing frailty of residents; unsuitable buildings; shortage of staff; constantly rising costs; trade union pressures and so on. In the end, however, the quality of life in a home depends on the quality of staff who run it. Pride and independence in residents can only be fostered if there is pride and independence in the staff – and not only the officer in charge and the care staff, but also the domestics, the cook and the gardener. With the residents they are creating a home just as truly as all the members of a family create the home in which they live, and unless this concept becomes a reality, no amount of theoretical emphasis on 'residents' rights' is likely to bear fruit in practice.

The creation of such an atmosphere depends on the guidance and encouragement which staff get from their employers (whether a local authority, a voluntary committee or a private owner), on the training which they receive and on the status which is attached to their job and which is reflected in pay and conditions of service. As long as residential care of the elderly is perceived as a second-class occupation which provides 'warehousing' for 'geriatrics' and does not require professional skills or offer adequate reward, those who work in this field will pass on their sense of uselessness and rejection to residents. However much domiciliary care improves there will always be those who simply cannot manage for themselves or who do not wish to do so. The best examples of residential care show how much can be done to make the last years of such people's lives positive and fulfilling, rather than withdrawal into a despairing apathy. It *can* be creative and fulfilling work.

However, such efforts do always raise the question of what the right course is when residents themselves resist having to make any effort or carry any responsibility. If an individual wants to be dependent, passive and immobile, how far should he be urged, cajoled, pushed or bullied in activity? This issue was raised by Roger Clough in an article in *Social Work Today*. He began by quoting another article in *The Guardian* which was entitled 'Elderly not ill-treated':

Elderly people at an old folk's home, many in their nineties, were made by staff to stagger unaided from meal tables. Sometimes it took them ten minutes to get to their feet. On other occasions they were left on the floor.

Yet their treatment did not amount to cruelty. Instead it was part of a deliberate rehabilitation technique to encourage residents to stay active.

41

Clough goes on to suggest that rehabilitation, though an acceptable goal in much social work and medicine, may not be appropriate in residential homes for the elderly. There are, he points out, dilemmas in treatment:

> Who profits from the treatment? Who decides that it is necessary? As a rule of thumb, treatment regimes should not be imposed on unwilling residents. The power of staff is great and consequently there is a need to guard against thoughtlessly translating their ideas into practice. I have heard of butter being replaced by margarine (it's better for their health) and cups of tea available to those who walked to the dining room. Whether these examples are regarded as cruel or not, a resident should have the right to eat butter, even though there are dangers in cholesterol; to remain inactive and lose the use of limbs. (After all, males over 35 face risks of epidemic proportions from coronary disease; but diets that are free from salt and daily jogging are not yet compulsory.) Like other individuals, the elderly in residential homes should be able to refuse treatment and live with the consequences.[3]

This is a basic issue which needs more attention than it has received. One basic concept which may help is that of 'normalisation' in the provision of residential care. This concept was developed in relation to the mentally handicapped and was then extended to general psychiatry. It is, however, applicable to those suffering from dementia and to the physically disabled of any age. As described by Edgar Miller in *Abnormal ageing – the psychology of senile and presenile dementia*:

> In outline, normalisation is two things. Firstly it gives a goal, this goal is that of achieving a lifestyle and pattern of behaviour that is as near the society norm for the afflicted individual's peers as possible . . . The other aspect of normalisation is that it is a principle of management. In simple outline it involves keeping those needing special care within an environment that is as close as can be achieved to the normal environment. It must be

presumed that the normal environment acts so as to maintain normal patterns of behaviour and it can be confidently expected that abnormal environments are likely to produce abnormal behaviour. Normalisation therefore places a very heavy stress on trying to ensure that handicapped individuals live in the community wherever possible. Where community living cannot be maintained, institutional living units must be designed by using society's normal living units as a model.

When the patient comes into residential care this should ideally have certain features. Normal old people do not normally live in large, sex segregated living units far from the usual residential areas and in which special management personnel e.g. nurses, make every-day decisions for them (what to eat, when to eat, when to bath, etc.). In contrast the ideal living units should be small, have the sexes integrated and be situated within the usual residential areas of the community. They should ensure the maximum participation of residents in running their daily lives. A further implication of this last point is that staff levels should be kept to a minimum and this is a view which contrasts with the perennial complaint that there are never anything like enough primary care staff to go round. More staff are presumably needed so as better to order residents' lives for them and it is not implausible that an excess of staff is likely to destroy rather than maintain any residual capacity for independent functioning that the residents might still retain. It must also be allowed that, in the case of a condition like dementia which is marked by a slow deterioration, there will have to be a steady transfer of control of his life from the patient to those taking care of him. The normalisation principle stresses that this transfer should be as slow as possible and not accelerated by a situation which actually encourages his ever increasing dependence.[4]

The practical implications of pursuing such a policy will include emphasis on maintaining as much self-care and independence as possible when people enter a home, so that the responsibilities and skills which they are able to exercise are not lost unnecessarily. 'Normalisation' also implies that residents should continue to maintain their customary involvement in the community – the pub, the church and the polling booth – as well as visiting friends and relatives. Once these external interests and activities are lost, it is almost impossible to get them started again.

Another practice which merits attention is the idea of a written contract which would be agreed when a resident comes into a home. This has its dangers, because if 'rights' in homes are the same as for any citizen anywhere, any reduction or restriction which really is essential should be imposed only on a particular individual in particular circumstances. Also, 'blanket' statements about what residents may or may not do carry the danger of it being assumed that behaviour and activities which are not specifically permitted are banned. Nevertheless, there is a case for some kind of individual written contract which would be agreed when a resident comes into a home. This might set out any general restrictions or rules which the home believed to be necessary, *with the reason for them*, and would also spell out as a basic principle that the home concerned would never stop someone from making their own choices or doing something for themselves unless it was *clear* that the danger to themselves or others outweighed the loss of freedom to the individual: also, that if the person concerned was capable of understanding the risk to himself arising from going to the pub, locking his door, bathing himself, etc., and still wished to take it, he should do so. If this contract was agreed at the outset, and fully understood by residents, staff and relatives, obsession with safety first and the lurking fear of 'the coroner's court' (see p. 77) might be reduced. Such a contract would require authoritative support from employers, committee members, etc., if the care staff were to believe that it meant what it said, and be willing to carry it out.

One interesting attempt to draw up such a contract – though it is generalised rather than tailor-made for each resident – has been made by the East Sussex County Council and is printed as an appendix to this chapter. It is heartening that a local authority has had the courage to make such a statement – though how far it will succeed in carrying it out remains to be seen and the fact that it is necessary at all underlines again the way in which basic rights of elderly residents have been eroded in the past.

Through its Homes Advice service for voluntary and private homes, its close relationships with local authority service providers and its administration of Hayward grants for the modernisation of voluntary homes, NCCOP has become deeply involved in the problems and possibilities of improving standards of residential care for the elderly. We are especially concerned to ensure that right and proper emphasis on improving the quality and quantity of domiciliary care and providing proper support for caring friends and relatives is not seen as an alternative to raising the quality and quantity of residential provision. The two services are complementary. If homes can offer day and weekend care; temporary 'halfway' care on discharge from hospital; short-stay support in times of family crisis, temporary disability or other urgent need; and rehabilitation after bereavement, self-neglect or illness, they will become part of the supportive network which enables elderly people to stay independent for as long as possible and enables neighbours and friends to sustain a caring role. If they can give the very frail and the mentally or physically disabled, who can no longer cope in their own homes, a setting in which they are treated as recognised and respected individuals, each with a long and complex personal history, and each with emotional needs and personal tastes, hopes, fears and foibles, they will become places in which old people are not 'put away', but can find a new and rewarding span of life.

Residents Rights

What you have a right to expect if you live in one of the County Council's homes for elderly people.

I. Basic rights of residents

1. The main concern of our homes will be the quality of life of their residents.
2. Residents have the right to personal independence, personal choice, and personal responsibility for their own actions.
3. Residents have the right to care for themselves as far as they are physically and mentally able, and willing, to do so.
4. Residents have the right to have their personal dignity respected by others in every way possible, and to be treated, whatever their disabilities or frailties, as individuals in their own right.
5. Residents have the right to personal privacy, for themselves their belongings and their affairs.
6. Residents have the right to take a full part in decisions about daily living arrangements, to be consulted about any changes which may be proposed, and to have a genuine say in social services policies.
7. Residents have the right to the same access to facilities and services in the surrounding community as any other citizen, including registration with the medical practitioner and dentist of their choice.
8. Residents have the right to be given every opportunity of mixing with other people in the community, whether by going out or by inviting other people in.
9. Residents have the right to have their cultural, religious, sexual and emotional needs accepted and respected as well as the whole range of other commonly accepted needs.
10. Residents have the right to expect management and staff to accept the degree of risk that is involved in these principles, and not to have their personal independence unnecessarily or unreasonably restricted for fear of such risk.

II. Some practical applications of these rights

1. Coming to live in a home

You will be able to make an introductory visit to the home and see round it before coming to live in it, unless ill health or an emergency makes this impossible. Whenever possible a member of staff of the home will visit you in your own home, or if need be in hospital, to discuss the change in advance and answer questions, and so that you can get to know each other.

Social Services will give you the fullest possible information about life in the particular home in which you will live, and each home will produce an individual brochure describing its particular features.

2. Rules and Routines

Unnecessary rules and practices, such as getting people up too early or obliging them to go to bed before they want to, will be discontinued. Daily routines will be as flexible and natural as possible, and above all designed to meet the needs and comfort of residents rather than other considerations. The overall aim will be a relaxed and comfortable atmosphere, with plenty of activity going on for those who want it.

3. Visiting

Visiting by relatives and friends is completely welcome, and no restrictions will be placed on this, unless of course you particularly request this. You will be able to see your visitors in complete privacy if you wish. Wherever possible there will be facilities for you to make tea or provide refreshments for your visitors.

4. Belongings

So long as there is enough space available, you will be able to bring your own articles of furniture and personal belongings into the home. Cupboards or drawers will be provided for residents to lock away personal belongings if they so wish.

5. Sharing of Rooms

Two or more people sometimes have to share a room because of the way the older homes are designed and the great demand for places. Sometimes however people share a room because they prefer to have companionship. We would like to make it unnecessary for anyone to share who doesn't want to, and in particular to do away with rooms having more than two beds. At present it is hard to achieve this because it would mean losing a lot of badly needed places, but we intend to do all we can to make things better.

6. Living in small groups

In several of our homes experiments have been made, with the agreement of the residents concerned, in grouping small numbers of people together for daily living purposes, with their own shared sitting-room and dining-room facilities. We would propose to encourage such developments in homes where residents and staff wish it, provided that the premises can be made suitable.

7. Making decisions and discussing policies

Residents will have a regular say in the everyday running of the home, whether by residents' meetings or representative committees. Opportunitites will be given in these meetings for suggestions and complaints to be made.

A Divisional Residents' Consultative Committee will be established to meet regularly with the Divisional Director. The Committee will be composed of representatives from each of the homes and will have the right to discuss all matters of policy and practice affecting the interests of residents, and to be consulted on any proposed changes.

The Annual Conference of residents representing all homes which has been successfully held for the past two years will be continued.

8. Complaints

The brochure for each home will include an explanation of your right to have any complaints heard by the officer-in-charge, and if satisfaction is not obtained, by a more senior divisional officer. The brochure will inform you how formal complaints should be registered.

Residents will also be kept informed of the name and address of the local Member of Parliament and the County and District Councillors for the ward in which the home is situated, so that they may approach any of these directly if they should desire it.

9. Care staff

Officers-in-charge will expect care staff to spend a reasonable part of their working time in personal contact with residents. Pressure of domestic and practical tasks sometimes makes this difficult to achieve, but it is emphasised that social contact with residents is an important part of the everyday work of all care staff.

10. Reviews

When you have been resident for some three months we plan to review, with your help, how you are getting on and whether your needs are being met. After that we will see that these things are considered at regular intervals, and that you continue to have plenty of opportunity to let us know what you think about it.

11. Mixed Homes

Our general aim is to make all homes capable of accommodating both men and women, and most of our homes are mixed already. Achieving this aim fully may take a long time because of the nature of some of the buildings we have, but in the meantime we will continue to try to give those who wish it a place in a mixed home. (What we can't do, unfortunately, is to guarantee you as many men as women, as there are always far more of the latter.)

PA/SMS
March 1979

REFERENCES

1. *Rights in residence*, Ed. D. Harris and J. Hyland, Residential Care Association, 1979.
2. *Residential care for the elderly in London*, Department of Health and Social Security, London, 1979.
3. R. Clough, 'No-one could call me a fussy man', *Social Work Today*, Vol. 9, No. 34, May 2, 1978.
4. E. Miller, *Abnormal ageing – the psychology of senile and presenile dementia*, John Wiley and Sons, 1977.

Human Rights and Nursing Care

Public hospitals are traditionally authoritarian institutions. Until the advent of scientific medicine, they were the resort of the poor – richer people being treated in their own homes. Their inmates carried the treble stigma of being the recipients of charity, physically weak and socially incompetent. They were therefore expected to be suitably grateful and obedient. This aura of the workhouse still lingers on in all hospitals, but it is strongest and hardest to dispel in the longstay institutions caring for the disabled, mentally ill, mentally handicapped and elderly. And, even leaving aside the geriatric wards, a high proportion of the residents in these institutions are old.

The point has been well made in an article in the *Lancet*:

> We are still trying to run our health and social services, for elderly people especially, in ways that stem from compulsion and custody, as in the past. We admit patients to hospital and discharge them; we even order them to hospital; we hold or detain them in hospital; we release them from hospital. This is the language of prison, of the police, and of the criminal law – not of hospitality.
>
> The Poor Laws may have disappeared in 1948 and with them the relieving officer and the workhouse, but the workhouse seems to have disappeared in name only: the same buildings used for much the same purpose, now called hospitals or welfare homes; and the attitudes associated with the Poor Laws are still strong – that is, relegation and less eligibility.[1]

All institutions have to have rules in order to facilitate the attainment of their primary object (in this case, healing and rehabilitation), make administration possible and minimise conflict between residents or patients. Entry into an institution, as was noted in the previous chapter, implies a surrender of some autonomy for the sake of the services which the institution can render. In many longstay hospitals, however, the rules inhibit both the autonomy of patients and the therapeutic purpose of the institution, since it is essential for successful rehabilitation that the patients find themselves as people. If the patient is to re-establish himself in the community, it is vital that he should be enabled to maintain or regain his identity, and because of his disorientation when moved away from his familiar support systems, the elderly patient needs especial help in this respect. Yet what happens in practice? The patient is labelled like a piece of luggage (even in the longstay wards) and even then often not correctly addressed by name and title. As one observer has said, 'from the point of view of maintaining identity, it cannot help if a grandmother is consistently addressed as "Miss" or a venerable maiden lady as "Granny".'

Choice in what we eat is a basic exercise in autonomy – energetically exercised by most two-year-olds – but one senior nurse states that in his experience:

> Breakfast is almost always tea, toast and porridge. Lunch, which should be a high point in the patient's day, is often the most boring. Many patients eat minced beef every day of the year simply because we do not have sufficient staff to supervise and assist with meals. It can be argued that it is dangerous to give the patient fried steak as he may asphyxiate on a large portion. However, even with limited ward staff, surely the diet could be more varied, for example, diced chicken, creamed fish, braised meats and other soft foods. The evening meal often consists of scrambled eggs for those who cannot easily swallow.
>
> In one ward I observed that at least six patients had minced beef for dinner and scrambled eggs for tea every day for six weeks.[2]

Even when menus giving choice of food are provided, these are often filled up by the ward clerk without consulting patients. Helping patients to complete menus could surely be an opportunity for daily one-to-one contact, where a volunteer could be most effectively used.

Choice of time to sleep is another very basic aspect of autonomy – refused only to young children, prisoners undergoing brainwashing and people in institutional care. Hospital patients are often woken between 6.30 and 7 a.m. at the end of the night shift of nurses, and are then kept sitting up until about 4 p.m. when the day shift put them to bed before they go off duty. The normal pattern for many elderly people would be much later rising – perhaps not till 9 or 10 a.m. – a nap lying down after lunch, and bed when they felt tired at night – perhaps not till quite late after watching a television programme which was not, like the daytime programmes, geared to children or football addicts. Such a regime would produce a more natural sleep pattern and therefore less need for sedatives, but all too often it is not achieved.

Control of money is a basic adult function. NCCOP has already drawn the attention of the Royal Commission on the National Health Service

> to the anomalies in the system whereby pensioners are required to give up earned benefit in return for long-term medical and nursing care with no resulting benefit to the hospitals which have to provide such care. Retirement pensions for which full contributions have been paid are normally reduced to £7·80 after a pensioner with no dependent wife or child has been in hospital for eight weeks and after one year only £3·90 of the pension can be received by the sick person (June 1979 figure); the remainder is paid to dependants if there are any, and otherwise withheld altogether unless re-settlement grant is required. Similar rules apply to other forms of pension and sickness benefit. The *rationale* for this is stated to be that 'National Insurance benefits are intended to help with ordinary needs at home. While in hospital some of these needs, such as food, are being met by the National Health Service and benefits are therefore reduced.'

The Corporation pointed out that these longstay elderly patients were being asked to forego income with no consequent benefit to the health service in general or to the geriatric hospitals in particular, and that they were therefore simultaneously paying a substantial part of their income for their care and suffering some of the worst conditions in the health service.

But it is by no means axiomatic that elderly patients will receive even the £3·90 due to them. The HAS Report for 1974 says:

> Hospitals accommodating longer stay elderly patients often hold the pension books of a proportion of patients and draw the pensions so that the patients may have cash if they wish. In some hospitals few patients draw any spending money; in others, with similar categories of patient, nearly all do so. Even in different wards of the same hospital there may be wide variation in the proportion of those entitled who draw any spending money. It appears that the variation may be due in part to the view taken by the senior ward staff, naturally concerned at the trouble, and indeed blame, they anticipate as a result of cash being mislaid and lost by elderly, possibly confused patients. Having even small sums of spending money is an important element of a patient's independence and indeed dignity. The facility to use money, once lost, is not easily regained. The very real risk of the loss of small sums is more than outweighed by the benefit having money can bring. It is very desirable that the health authorities should establish, as a matter of policy, that small sums should be held by elderly patients whenever possible, and all reasonable risk of loss be accepted. The emphasis should be changed from a decision having to be taken as to which patients should draw money to a decision as to which patients should not.

It is five years since that was written, but even now how often is it followed as a routine practice? How often are patients encouraged to buy from a mobile shop or acquire personal possessions? In one hospital a clerk goes round every two weeks telling each person how much they have to their credit and

54

discussing with them what they would like to spend it on – perhaps a small personal TV or radio, presents for relatives, a bottle of port or brandy, or a taxi ride round the town? If this can be done in one hospital – why not in others? Again, volunteers could play a useful role here.[3]

Intrusive, uncontrollable noise invades personality. Noise is used as an instrument of torture in brainwashing. But elderly people parked in day rooms are often subject to non-stop television and even in bed, may have 'leaking' piped radio music coming at them as well as the cries of disturbed patients; if they are wearing hearing aids such background noise becomes still more intolerable. W. Raphael has found from her opinion survey of the views of longstay old people in hospitals that noise was the most frequently complained-about problem.[3]

Suitable, attractive, dignified clothing is another basic element in human dignity and this has been widely recognised, but many hospitals, and especially those using a centralised laundry system, are still not able to provide and care for the personal clothing of longstay elderly people. As one ward sister said:

In spite of DHSS policy issued in 1972 requiring as a minimum standard that personal clothing service and laundry should be provided in longstay areas, the introduction of this vital provision has been appallingly slow nationally. Psychiatry has clearly grasped the morale boosting and rehabilitative advantages to be gained and has forged ahead with introduction into the field of their longstay patients. Sadly though, it would appear the need in the field of the elderly has not been afforded the same priority, or are we just less vocal! – or do these people, as a century ago, still deserve only second hand consideration and clothes.

At present a variety of provision exists in our hospitals ranging from a first class fully personalised service, to the other extreme where so little thought has been given to the matter that very nearly all longstay patients exist from morning till night in night shirts, night dresses or pyjamas (the one frequently indistinguishable from the other!).

In mixed units especially, lack of clothing provision causes much embarrassment. Conveniently split hospital night dresses prove unbecoming when making one's way across a day room in full view of all, and the gentlemen's pyjamas commonly have no buttons to the jackets or trousers. One wouldn't dare to estimate the incidents of 'indecent exposure' that occur all too easily, the excuse of having no service can become the crutch for nursing staff who in time themselves become forgetful or indifferent to personal pride and privacy. The next move down the slippery slope is that the patients themselves become indoctrinated to forget these finer elements and the pattern of regression rather than progression becomes established.[4]

Numerous other examples of ways in which elderly patients are deprived of identity, dignity and autonomy can be provided – especially in washing arrangements and the use of lavatories and commodes. The reasons given for such treatment are usually out-of-date buildings, inadequate facilities and shortage of staff. However, apart from the difficulties arising from inadequate sanitary facilities, none of the forms of deprivation cited above relate to building design, or the provision of expensive extra facilities. As for staff, there certainly are real difficulties in recruitment and allocation, and it is true that encouraging as much independence as possible can be more time-consuming than treating people as bodies to be dressed, washed and fed. However, even if wards are fully staffed, the kind of care given does not necessarily improve because expectations of what can be done are too low and the whole system is geared to minimal care with very few staff. Also, what staff are available are not always used as positively as possible, or encouraged to develop skills in maintaining mobility, communicating with the deaf, encouraging conversation and personal activity, reinforcing awareness of present reality, etc. If the job was seen as a positive one, perhaps more people would be willing to do it.

The whole ethos of nursing care is directed towards protection from harm, and accidents are therefore felt to be a disgrace, especially if they occur in a ward which is not geared to a programme of planned, active rehabilitation where a degree of risk may be accepted. All accidents have to be reported to the senior nurse and an accident form completed in triplicate. If the accident proves fatal, there will be a coroner's inquest and this is especially dreaded. This may not be realistic so far as the actual role of the coroner is concerned (see p. 77) but it is certainly true that a fatal accident to an elderly person in hospital is likely to produce adverse publicity in the local press and will not promote the career of the nurse in charge at the time. It requires a really positive approach from the consultant and the hospital administrator (who may fear claims from relatives) to militate against a 'safety first' policy.

The consequence is that confused and unsteady patients may be literally imprisoned by the use of cotsides and 'geriatric chairs' and in some cases be physically tied down. The routine use of cotsides is now widely disapproved of by geriatricians as increasing the danger to restless, confused, or independent-minded patients who will try to climb over them. This opinion is reinforced by the findings of a study of hospital accidents with special reference to old people carried out in a group of Scottish hospitals. This reported:

> Fourteen out of the 43 falls out of bed occurred when cotsides were in place and in all of these, the patient was suffering from restless confusion. Few could question the need for cotsides for ill patients and those recovering from an anaesthetic, who are in danger of rolling out of bed, but their use in restless, confused patients is more debatable. They are easily climbed over and around and the distance fallen may then be greater than it would otherwise have been. To the confused patient, the feeling of being caged in may be an added encouragement to 'escape'. Both Davidson (1975) and Isaacs (1965) have condemned their use in this type of patient. Restlessness in a confused patient is, in any case, a symptom requiring investigation, not restraint, pain, the desire to micturate or defecate, anoxia and the toxic effect of drugs being frequent causes. Perhaps one valid argument in favour of cotsides is that their rattling at night is an effective

alarm system where, as frequently happens, only one nurse is looking after a ward.[5]

Nevertheless, many nurses feel safer when they are up and will replace them when they get a chance.

The kind of chair which keeps a patient immobilised, either by making it too low for him to get out of unaided, or by penning him in by placing a fixed tray across his lap, or by tilting him back at an angle, is equally deplored by the experts and in equally common use – even to the point of being advertised in the journal of the British Geriatric Society *Age and Ageing*. (The writer knew personally one elderly woman who was imprisoned in such a chair for three years and who cried with frustration about it each time she was visited. True, she might have fallen if she had tried to stand and walk unaided though she could do so when she entered the hospital. But would this really have been a worse fate?)

In general, the official attitude to accidents in hospital seems to be very negative. The Edinburgh study quoted above found that the accident report forms which have to be completed are medico-legal in function, listing witnesses, recording details of injury and attempting to define responsibility. The study found there was virtually no medical examination directed towards finding causes of falls although other studies of accidents have shown a high incidence of medical precipitating factors, many of which are at least partially remediable. Also the accident report frequently puts responsibility for the accident on the failure of a confused patient to follow instructions. As the author of the study says:

> It seems futile to put responsibility on a patient with limited memory for discharging casually given instructions. Reinforcing instructions by referring 'at risk' patients to the physiotherapy or occupational therapy department of the hospital for safety and fall training is, however, worthwhile. Totally negative instructions banning all activity on the part of the patient, as occurred on a number of the accident forms, can hardly be justified. Apart from the fact that such instructions are only rarely adhered to, this attitude ultimately leads back to the

pre-war care of the elderly, with wards full of patients kept bedfast for their own good.

It is of interest that the DHSS has made it a specific policy to encourage greater freedom and responsibility for mentally ill and mentally handicapped patients, and the Health Service Commissioner has accepted that this must involve greater risk. In his report for 1977–8 he says:

> During the year I have received several complaints involving the supervision of patients in hospitals for the mentally ill and mentally handicapped. These complaints arise either where the patient has been free to leave the hospital at will and has suffered some misfortune whilst away from the protection of the hospital; or where an incident has occurred in the hospital which the patient's relatives consider could have been avoided had there been a greater degree of supervision by the staff.
>
> There are several factors which affect the degree of supervision which is either desirable or possible in these circumstances. In 1964 the Department of Health and Social Security asked hospital authorities to review their policies with regard to the care of the mentally ill and to concentrate on providing an environment in which the patients are responsible for their own actions. This entailed a relaxation of the former custodial system and the abolition of the visible trappings of protection such as locked doors.
>
> If patients who are not considered to be a danger to themselves or others are to live a reasonably normal life they must be given some degree of freedom and for the great majority this gives them a sense of fulfilment and dignity and very little risk attaches to it. But there is inevitably some risk. In the following three cases the patients died in tragic circumstances, but I found no grounds for criticism of hospital staffs for any lack of supervision.

The cases cited were: a young man (an informal patient) who was admitted to a non-secure psychiatric unit after an attempted suicide but succeeded in committing suicide; a mentally handi-capped epileptic woman who absconded with a male patient and was found in a derelict house two weeks later, having died of asphyxia caused by an epileptic fit; and a schizophrenic 16-year-old boy who disappeared from the adolescent unit where he had been a patient for several months and was found drowned in a local reservoir.

In every case it was felt that the legal rights of the patients and need for 'as normal a life as possible' justified the risk.[6] If this is true for mentally ill and handicapped people, it must be equally true for the old.

It is not only institutional tradition, old buildings, shortage of staff and fear of accidents which detract from the quality of life 'enjoyed' by old people in longstay wards. There are indications of more deeply rooted contradictions and tensions in geriatric nursing which affect the kind of care the patients receive and produce double-messages in the communications which they are offered.

One of these conflicts is between the message 'we can help you to become independent if you really want to try' and 'we are here to look after you' – a conflict which a Tavistock Report describes as follows:

> Geriatric patient care requires a constant effort to identify and foster the patient's motivation to get better; and to some degree this means ignoring his overt or covert pleas to be dependent and looked after. Nurses through their training and professional culture are particularly prone to pick up these pleas and to find them difficult to resist. They are then placed in a bind: to resist is to be callous, to respond may be inimical to the patient's recovery. Nurses are likely to defend themselves against this conflict by displacing the callousness on to the doctors, leaving themselves with the conviction that they would be tender and responsive if only the doctors allowed them to be.
>
> In addition, of course, the communities from which the staff members come are the same as, or similar to, those of the patients. Staff are carriers of the value

systems of those communities and to the extent that the values are in conflict with the concept of progressive patient care, that conflict confronts the staff. This will make it the more difficult for them to be unequivocal over reinforcing the patient's often fragile motivation to get better. Instead they may collude, perhaps unconsciously, with his helplessness and dependency.

The culture of the nursing profession may also contribute to this. It is a culture which is more favourable to dependency than to fostering independence. For example, the fact that a nurse has little or no authority to exercise discretion in her treatment of the patient is hardly conducive to her encouraging him to act independently. As the word itself implies, it is the role of patient to be passive. In the setting of the general hospital, where the patient himself is usually highly motivated to get better and get out, this may not matter; but in a geriatric hospital, where motivation is weak or ambivalent, the nursing culture may run counter to the task. Although the nurse may overtly endorse progressive patient care, she may have to fight hard against the cultural influences if she is to avoid encouraging dependency by her actual behaviour. And she is then in the position of fighting against what is an important source of professional support for her in a demanding job.[7]

A further problem is that staff in a rehabilitation ward may be forced to give different messages to different patients within hearing of each other. If one person is being persuaded to accept a bed in the longstay ward, its characteristics will be described as positively as possible to him. If another is being persuaded that he really wants to go home and can and should achieve sufficient independence to do so, the message will be 'the long stay ward is an awful place – you don't want to go there, do you?' Moreover, staff may themselves be uncertain how much rehabilitation is possible. There is very little scientific evidence about diagnosing maximum capacity so the tendency as one senior nurse described it to the writer is 'to bully and see what happens'. As was noted above, this can be distressing to nurses.

Confusion over treatment goals may be still more serious in the longstay wards. The patients in these wards represent the hospital's failures. They have not been cured or rehabilitated sufficiently to enable discharge and they have not died. Their existence is antagonistic to the ethos of the hospital – hence derogatory descriptions like 'bed-blockers' and 'crumblies'.

Nursing staff on these wards tend to have less prestige than those in acute or rehabilitation units and are sometimes seen as less efficient. This may be because if staff are short, the more efficient individuals will be selected for the more obviously demanding jobs. If this happens a vicious circle of low morale, poor staff and difficulties in recruitment can be set up.

Although patients in these wards are not expected to make any real improvement, they are, because they are still in hospital, still subject to medical direction with its implicit goal of treatment and its primary goal of saving life. It is very difficult for doctors and nurses in this situation to shed their drive towards these goals and concentrate instead on providing the best quality of life which is possible in the hospital environment, and the final achieving of a peaceful, accepted and pain-free death. It is harder still if the longstay wards also include patients for whom there is still hope for rehabilitation, even if at a very slow pace.

One of the problems in writing this section of the report has been that the points made in it are already well known to the point of tedium. Again and again, publications such as the DHSS's *In-patients' day*, the King's Fund's *Living in hospital*, the RCN/BGS's *Improving geriatric care in hospital*, and indeed NCCOP's own *Investigation of nursing problems in hospital*, way back in 1962, have made exactly the same points. But exhortation is not enough to produce sustained better standards as a steering committee in the Exeter Health District found when it tried to implement the guidelines published in the RCN/BGS working party report. So, instead of 'urging staff to be somehow better people', they divided the guidelines into appropriate sections and asked administrative, medical and nursing staff to comment on them and arrive at a consensus which should be applied in the district. This was followed by allocation of reponsibility for policy decisions and implementation at each appropriate level and the development of a programme of indoctrination and training for each nurse on the ward floor, using existing training facilities. This imaginative yet practical and down-to-earth approach to changing actual behaviour is what we need, but it is still too rare.[8] It is true that in the teaching units, and where there are dedicated medical or ward staff, things have improved – but what of the back wards of the geriatric or general hospitals up and down the country? An almost desperate medical social worker in a Lancashire mill town told the writer:

> In practical terms the old people have no rights at all and no effective means of protest or real choice. If they insist on going home and later have to come back, they get a poorer standard of treatment as being non-cooperative. They are afraid of a comeback if they complain and anyway tradition is against it. In any case the complicated complaints system means that it is very difficult to produce effective and constructive complaints and by the time a complaint has gone up the echelon it is always someone else's fault. Relatives' clinics here do not include real discussion of the problem on level terms – they just boil down to saying when the patient is coming home. Life on the wards is very stultifying – one day room with a budgie in the corner, constant telly, no time to talk with staff or real contact with them, no use of volunteers. The OTs refuse to do diversional therapy, but no one else will do it either. There are no means of practising daily living skills on the wards, so that patients deteriorate and when a residential place does come up, they are not fit to go.

Constant reiteration of what is wrong seems to have little effect, perhaps because, as was noted above, NHS hospital staff are just not geared to provide long-term nursing care. As one geriatrician said:

> No one is trying to rethink what we are doing in the long-stay wards or to rebalance the budget allocations. At present we are spending £10,000 a week on 100 longstay patients and if you increase the standards of care you increase costs.

63

He saw his own role as 'a cross between a scientific doctor and the master of a workhouse', 'giving the poor the service which the rich can buy' and 'using old isolation plant for isolating the elderly at a cost of £1m a year'.

Perhaps it is basically impossible to maintain human dignity in longstay hospitals and we should be looking much harder at alternatives in terms of community nursing homes and community domiciliary nursing?

REFERENCES

1. F. Allen Binks, 'Changing the subject' in the *Lancet*, July 1, 1978, p. 23.
2. J. G. Orr, 'Care of the elderly patient in hospital', *Nursing Times*, Vol. 73, No. 27, July 7, 1977.
3. W. Raphael and J. Mandeville, *Old people in hospital*, King Edward's Hospital Fund for London, 1979.
4. *Report of a workshop on the diffiuclties of implementing a personal clothing policy for long stay patients and possible solutions*, University of Manchester Department of Geriatric Medicine and the Disabled Living Foundation, November 1977.
5. C. J. Scott, 'Accidents in hospital with special reference to old people', *Health Bulletin*, Vol. 34, No. 6, November 1976. The references given in the text are to R. Davidson (1975) Practitioner, 215,600 and B. Isaacs (1965) *An introduction to geriatrics*, London, Baillière, Tindall and Cassell.
6. Health Service Commissioner, Annual Report for 1977–1978, HMSO 1978.
6. T. C. C. Dartington, P. J. Jones and E. J. Miller, *Geriatric hospital care*, The Tavistock Institute of Human Relations, 1974. (unpublished).
8. J. Cruise, 'Better geriatric care: making it happen', *Health Trends*, Vol. 10, No. 4, November 1978, Department of Health and Social Security.

Consent to Treatment and 'The Right to Die'

The advent of sophisticated life support systems, crash resuscitation techniques and other methods of holding off death has given rise to a good deal of public debate about the point at which it is right to discontinue active treatment of a dying or 'vegetable' patient and the extent to which the patient's own wishes concerning treatment should be respected.* This chapter therefore looks more closely at what 'consent' to treatment means and how it is obtained and discusses some of the ethical and social factors which influence the kind of care which a dying elderly person receives.

The Medical Defence Union states the legal position on consent thus: 'A person suffering from a disease or injury is not normally bound to submit himself to medical treatment or even to consult a doctor if he does not wish to do so' and the Union warns that treatment without consent could lead to an action for damages.[1] But what does 'consent' mean? To start with, it must be 'informed' – that is the nature and purpose of the treatment should have been properly explained.

One wonders how often an effort is made to provide elderly people with information at sufficient depth to make consent 'informed' in any real sense. There is certainly some evidence that patients of any age group who are admitted to hospital are liable to feel that they are not given adequate information about their illness and its treatment. For example, an investigation of

*This is quite a different matter from voluntary euthanasia or assisted suicide which involve not only the stopping of active treatment but the deliberate hastening of the patient's death. This is illegal when treating people of any age and is therefore irrelevant to a discussion of situations in which elderly people are discriminated against.

100 patients at the Bristol Royal Infirmary found that 55 of them were dissatisfied with what they had been told and the way in which ward rounds were conducted. They felt that the intelligence of patients was under-rated and disliked the way in which they were excluded from discussion by doctors who muttered among themselves at the end of the bed, using incomprehensible medical jargon. (This may have been necessary for teaching purposes, but if so, this does not seem to have been explained to the patients and an alternative time provided for answering questions about their illness and treatment.)

If this is the experience of a random selection of patients, it is likely to be still more the experience of elderly people in hospital who, as the survey found, were even more reluctant than other age groups to ask questions because they were in awe of the doctor and felt, 'it was not their place to ask'. Open wards, which make private communication difficult, the number of people on a ward round, and deafness, also inhibit communication, as does pressure of time and lack of training in communication. However, it is worth noting that some 10% of the patients interviewed and particularly the elderly, wanted to know little or nothing about their illness. An 83-year-old woman said,

I leave my life in their hands, and let them do what they want to do. After all, it's for my own good.[2]

The patient must not only be informed but be mentally competent to make a decision. As I. M. Kennedy puts it:

A patient who is conscious and refuses further treatment must have his wish respected, whatever his condition, provided he is mature and lucid enough to make such a decision. If the doctor thinks the patient is not sufficiently lucid or mature, then the decision should be ignored.[3]

This surely is a crucial issue when treating confused or dying elderly people. At what point is a doctor justified in deciding that a person is not 'lucid', and that his expressed wishes are not valid? And at what point does passive resistance become refusal to consent? Dr A. A. Baker in a taped talk used for teaching purposes cites as an example an elderly woman who was failing to recover after an operation and refused to eat. She was then fed by tube and when she tried to tear the tubes out, her arms were tied down. She died in that condition. Leaving aside the question as to whether tube feeding was in any case a 'heroic measure' which was not justified in keeping alive a person of this age (a question which is further discussed below) should the woman's refusal to co-operate have been taken as a refusal to consent? Kennedy acknowledges that the doctor is final arbiter of the crucial question as to whether the patient is lucid and 'understands the nature and implications of the decision and is competent to make it.' He also points out that the decision is made harder by the knowledge that most terminally ill patients are receiving medication and may be suffering pain and distress, all of which could affect their mental competence, quite apart from the doctor's reluctance to withdraw treatment. 'Ultimately,' Kennedy says, 'the good faith of the doctor must guide his actions.'

Consent must also be 'fully and freely given', and this may be difficult to achieve since, as Berkowitz points out, an elderly person may be subject to all sorts of pressures to give consent, from his doctor, his relatives or care staff on whom he is dependent.[4]

Clearly, then, the concept of consent being required to legalise treatment does not solve a number of moral dilemmas when it is applied in practice – a point which Kennedy discusses at some length in a paper on the *Legal effect of requests by the terminally ill and aged not to receive further treatment from doctors*.[5] Here he suggests that the philosophical principle of the right to self-determination, which underlies the concept of consent, is undermined by an equally strong philosophical premise of paternalism whose basis, as he sees it, is that 'decisions concerning a particular person's fate are better made *for* him than *by* him' and that 'the law is constructed in such a way that very probably only the lucid and self-assertive patient who has a sympathetic and understanding doctor is able in most circumstances to have his own way and to be left alone in freedom to die. All other patients run the risk of having their wishes flouted'. He adduces a number of factors which combine to produce this result:

1. The determination of capacity to consent or withhold consent is not made by the patient but by those treating him. 'It is as if there existed a right to free speech but before exercising it

what was to be said had to be submitted for approval to someone who had a practically unchallengeable power of censorship.'

2. The healthy are likely to presume that no one really wants to die, so that a request that treatment should cease is seen as either the response to a passing mood or a loss of mental fitness and therefore a symptom of unsoundness of mind.

3. The doctor's professional training predisposes him to 'save' lives and treat the sick. 'Furthermore, modern medical training may well encourage him to see himself as a scientist applying particular skills to solve a problem rather than dealing with people. This takes on an added significance when it is remembered that geriatrics and the terminally ill are regarded as the failures of the health service and often consigned to the young and inexperienced who, as one doctor recently put it, 'do strive very officiously to keep people alive because they are interested scientifically and they want to use every method as part of their training'.[6]

Kennedy emphasises that he is not suggesting that there is a conspiracy on the part of doctors to deprive patients of their rights, or that doctors act out of ill-will. 'Rather, it is conceded that they doubtless act of a well-meaning desire to treat. What is suggested is that the supposed right to self-determination is not perhaps the creature it is thought to be.'

An interesting illustration of the whole problem is provided by a recent case in Florida which was reported in the *New Law Journal*:

A 73-year-old man who was mentally alert and aware of his situation was kept alive by means of a mechanical respirator attached to a breathing hole in his trachea. Even with this device his expectation of life was limited indeed and removing the equipment would probably result in death within an hour. On several occasions he had physically attempted to remove the respirator but had been prevented by hospital personnel. He then took the matter to court and asked that he should be allowed to determine himself whether his life should be continued by the extraordinary expensive and painful mechanical means now used. The court said that the medical profession should not substitute its judgment for the patient's and found as a matter of fact and law that no state of medical interest is sufficient to upset the patient's decision to decline any further life-prolonging treatment by extraordinary means. His right to privacy and his self-determination as to the course of his remaining natural life should not be over-ruled by the courts. The patient was free to leave the hospital whenever he deemed it expedient and his desires should not be frustrated by the hospital, the doctors or the state attorney. It followed, of course, that none of the hospital staff nor the state attorney should be subjected to any civil liability for failure to provide additional care and treatment.

The state attorney argued that any termination of treatment would be self-murder and that anybody assisting in such termination would be breaking the criminal law. The court said that the termination of extraordinary treatment was not homicide but was the result of the free exercise of a constitutional right of privacy. Death that follows would be from natural causes and not unlawful homicide. Anyone assisting a patient in the exercise of his right to privacy cannot be guilty of infringing the criminal law. (Pearlmutter v. Florida Medical Center. Florida Circuit Court. 17th Judicial Circuit. Broward County. July 11 1978).[7]

Many States in the USA have tried to deal with some of the problems outlined above concerning 'lucidity' and 'consent' by passing legislation which grants terminally-ill persons the right to authorise, by a prior directive to physicians (sometimes called a 'living will') the withdrawal of life sustaining procedures when death is believed to be imminent. The first and most famous of these Acts, on which most of the others have been based, is the California Natural Death Act.[8] The core words of the directive are as follows:

If at any time I should have an incurable injury, disease, or illness certified to be a terminal condition by two physicians, and where the application of life-sustaining procedures would serve only to artificially prolong the moment of my death, and where my physician determines that my death is imminent whether or not life-sustaining procedures are utilized, I direct that such procedures be withheld or withdrawn, and that I be permitted to die naturally.

For this directive to be legally valid, a mentally competent adult must have signed it before two witnesses (who are not related to him and will not benefit by his death) at least two weeks after he has received in writing a diagnosis from two physicians that he is suffering from a terminal illness. (The two-week gap is meant to ensure that he does not act on impulse when told of the diagnosis.) If, when the time comes for a decision to be made about withholding or withdrawing treatment, the patient is still able to communicate, the doctor must confirm that he still wishes treatment to be withdrawn. Even then, so far as action under this Act is concerned, the life sustaining procedures cannot be withheld or withdrawn if they would postpone death for a long time.

The Act has come in for some trenchant criticism, not only from those who fear (wrongly) that it opens the door to voluntary euthanasia or assisted suicide, but also from those who feel that the problems of eligibility, definition and interpretation which it poses are insurmountable and that the 'imminence of death' requirement excludes the most difficult cases where respirators and drip feeds can prolong life indefinitely.[9] Also it is argued that living wills enshrine into the law the false notion that without them, physicians are masters, not servants of their patients. 'Freedom of medical practice is impaired, and families are excluded on the false assumption that physicians generally resuscitate their patients to death, thereby imposing medicated indignities upon them . . . a patient who has made a living will may be under-resuscitated for fear of professional misconduct. . . . A patient who has made no such directive is likely to be over-resuscitated insofar as his not making one when he could is taken to signal of his wishes in the matter.'[10]

These arguments strengthen the case against passing any such legislation in the United Kingdom, although there is, of course, nothing to prevent individuals from making their wishes known in writing to their doctors and relatives. It is already clear that in the UK there is no obligation on a doctor, when a patient appears to be near death, to continue 'heroic' treatment which has no prospect of benefiting the patient. Kennedy states the position as he sees it thus:

An alternative, more common, term than 'heroic' is 'extraordinary'. It was Pope Pius XII (1957) who first advanced the view that doctors were not obliged to give, nor patients to accept, 'extraordinary medical measures'. The term has consistently been interpreted as meaning 'whatever here and now is very costly or very unusual or very painful or very difficult or very dangerous, or if the good effects that can be expected for its use are not proportionate to the difficulty and inconvenience that are entailed' (Church Assembly Board, 1965). An example of an extraordinary measure in the case of terminally ill would be a respirator where the patient can no longer breathe for himself. In his 1976 Stevens lecture, the Archbishop of Canterbury expressed his support for this as a moral principle. I take the view that it is also the legal principle. *Indeed, I would go so far as to say that a doctor who continued treatment past this point would be behaving at least unethically if not unlawfully* (present writer's italics).

A doctor's obligation, when he can no longer hold back the approach of death, is to make the patient comfortable, including easing his pain. If, to ease pain, the doctor must take measures which may hasten death, this is permissible, *provided the doctor's aim is only the relief of pain* (present writer's italics).

This reflects the so-called double effect theory and was incorporated into English law in one of the few decided cases in this area. R. v. Bodkin Adams (1957).[3]

The Dictionary of Medical Ethics spells this out in more detail:

It is the patient's ultimate interest which should determine the treatment he receives, that interest being seen in relation to his unique being and his unique human and social environment . . . having in mind not only his medical condition but also his spiritual and emotional capacity, his religious convictions, the degree of effective interaction between him and those nearest to him, his personal and social commitments and what can be afforded (by his family and by the State) on his behalf. . . .

'Ordinary' is what is normal, established, well-tried, of known effectiveness, within the resources and skills available, of calculable and acceptable risk; of generally low mortality; involving pain, disturbance and inconvenience all within predictable limits of acceptance and control; *and all proportionate to expected and lasting benefit to the patient* (present writer's italics). These procedures the patient has a right to require and the physician a duty to undertake.

'Extraordinary' means would include investigating and experimental procedures of uncertain efficacy, or even carrying a high mortality rate; those involving a heavy disporportion between the pain, mutilation or psychological disfigurement of the patient and any immediate long term benefit reasonable, predictable, or of disproportionate cost.

These extraordinary procedures, the author says, cannot be demanded by patient as of right and the physician has no duty to undertake them.[11]

Clearly, this whole issue is a complex and sensitive one in which legal definitions are of limited use, and personal judgement, skill and compassion are paramount. In the end, it is good practice and not legal theory which matters. Practice has certainly been greatly improved by the growth of the hospice movement with its concept of 'appropriate' treatment and the enabling of 'a good death', and the development of specialist skills in relieving pain without clouding consciousness. However, it is much easier to exercise a careful and humane judgement concerning the prolonging of life in a hospice for the dying, where the avowed object of the institution is to enable people to die well, than it is in a hospital where the principal avowed object is to treat disease. Even in hospital, it may be easier not to give active treatment in an acute admission ward than in a longstay ward. This is because staff can feel a measure of success in identifying a terminal illness and so can allow a terminal care regime to be set up. Also the nurses will be trained to keep an emotional distance, the staff are less likely to know the patients as individuals, and it is easier to foretell death when the illness is acute. On longstay wards the situation can be different because the nurses may become identified with an implied objective of looking after people in order to *prevent* death. In this situation the nurses are likely to have a close bond with the patient and they may find it difficult to agree that the point has been reached when 'tender loving care' should take over from treatment. The doctor who judges that the patient is dying may find that in effect the nursing staff reject his opinion.

There is, therefore, still a great need for medical and nursing staff to be trained to see the care of the dying as a positive form of care, demanding skill and sensitivity and there is a need also for better support to be given to staff to help them to cope with the emotional burden which is concomitant to such an approach. They need support too to help them deal sensitively with relatives and not to allow routine nursing tasks to drive relatives away, against their will, from a dying person's bedside. At present this happens all too often and there is little effective protest about it. As Helen Franks says in an article describing the death of her elderly mother-in-law:

A little later, and more wide-awake, she cried again, defenceless as a child. Two nurses came in, I said, 'Leave us a little, she will be quiet in a moment.' I was pushed aside – they had come to extract the saliva to ease her breathing. 'Yes, I know, but leave us a moment, please,' I said.

I was physically pushed from the bedside, and so I stood outside the small ward shaking with anger and pain at the waste of a precious moment, knowing excruciatingly that it was wrong.

The hospital was in the kind of area unused to the

outspoken middle-class. 'Let me explain,' I said to the senior nurse as she emerged. 'I do not wish to listen. I will not talk to you,' she replied. I stood and looked in at the grey figure on the bed. The pillows had been removed, the wrinkled head lay with eyes closed to the ceiling, mouth open, looking now like Munch's painting The Scream.

It was the last I saw of her. On the way out I saw the sympathetic doctor, the one with whom I'd talked of the dignity of dying.

Next morning they telephoned, at 6 a.m. She had died a quarter of an hour earlier. It had been peaceful, probably painless. But one of her last moments amongst the living had been sacrificed to routine and sheer insensitivity.

The elderly, like the very young, have no say in our society. But the young, unlike the elderly, have fierce protection from parents. They also have watchdog organisations like NAWCH (National Association for the Welfare of Children in Hospital) which has campaigned vigorously for parents' accessibility to children in hospital and a more sensitive approach to their needs. Will Age Concern, or Help the Aged or some similar body, help to do the same for the elderly and those relatives who support and are concerned for them?[12]

A strong lead from public opinion, combined with better training and support for medical and nursing staff, are all needed, but along with these is also the need for much more extensive domiciliary nursing and medical services, so that elderly people can die amongst friends and relatives in familiar surroundings with no subjection to hospital routine or danger of 'heroic' measures of treatment. That this can be done without causing too much stress to relatives is proved by the success of the domiciliary care teams sent out by the hospices for the dying and also by the Hospital at Home schemes.[13] This subject receives only cursory, almost off-hand mention in the Department of Health and Social Security's Discussion Document *A happier old age*. Much more information is required about the kind of

74

support which is needed by those who wish to die at home and how it can best be linked to present community and hospital nursing services. This is an issue which ought to be a focus of major attention in the Health Service in the immediate future.

REFERENCES

1. *Consent to treatment*, The Medical Defence Union, 1974.
2. Maureen Reynolds, 'No news is bad news: patient's views about communication in hospital', *British Medical Journal*, 1978, 1, 1673–1676.
3. I. McC. Kennedy, 'The law relating to the treatment of the terminally ill' in *The management of terminal disease*, ed. C. M. Saunders, Edward Arnold, 1978.
4. S. Berkowitz, 'Informed consent. Research on the Elderly', *The Gerontologist*, Vol. 18, No. 3, 1978.
5. I. McC. Kennedy, 'The legal effect of requests by the terminally ill and aged not to receive further treatment from doctors', *Criminal Law Review*, April 1976.
6. I. McC. Kennedy (ref 5) quoting from G. Williams, 'Euthanasia', *Medico Legal Journal*, No. 41.
7. *New Law Journal*, January 18, 1979.
8. California Health and Safety Code, div. 7, pt. 1, chap. 3.9, *Natural Death Act*. Secs. 7185–7195.
9. W. J. Winslade, 'Thoughts on technology and death: an appraisal of California's Natural Death Act', *De Paul Law Review*, Vol. 26, No. 4, Summer 1977.
10. P. Ramsay, 'Ethics at the edges of life', Yale University Press, 1978 summarising arguments presented by R. A. McCormick and A. E. Hellegers, 'Legislation and the living will', *America*, March 12 1977.
11. *Dictionary of Medical Ethics*, ed. A. S. Duncan, G. R. Dunstan and R. B. Welbourne, Darton Longman and Todd, 1977 (Extracts used by permission of the publisher).
12. H. Franks, 'A death without dignity', *The Guardian*, May 5 1979.
13. Stephen Cang, 'Why not hospital-at-home here?' *Age Concern Today*. No. 20. Winter 1976/77, pp. 9–11.

Fatal Accidents and the Role of the Coroner's Court

Very old age brings with it increased risk of accidental falls as a result of arthritis, bone weakness, dizziness, confusion and similar disabilities. When such falls do occur very old people may die as a result, either directly because of the injury, or indirectly through broncho-pneumonia, pulmonary embolism or deep vein thrombosis arising from immobilisation. Such deaths may be thought of as being as 'natural' as heart failure or they may be seen as a hazard against which old people should be defended, even at the cost of greatly limiting their freedom of movement (see pp. 56–59). One important factor which affects the way in which these deaths are regarded, especially by residential care and nursing staff, is the legal necessity of holding a formal coroner's inquest on all deaths arising from a fatal accident. This chapter therefore discusses what the role of the coroner is, and looks at possible changes in the law which might help to change attitudes to this kind of 'risk'.

The office of coroner is one of the oldest known in English law. Its original purpose was to protect the financial interests of the Crown, since the property of criminals could be confiscated. From this it followed that coroners had to ascertain whether criminal action had caused violent or unnatural death and all such deaths had to be reported to him. He then held an inquest with the assistance of a local jury and if someone was indicted of homicide by the inquest, could issue a warrant for the suspected person's arrest.

Over the years, the coroner's role has changed radically. He is still responsible for ascertaining circumstances and cause of death, whenever a doctor who attended the case recently cannot certify that it was caused by some specified disease, or a death is 'violent or otherwise unnatural'. But the object of this enquiry is *not to apportion blame*, but to give the Registrar enough information to enable him to register the death and to ascribe it to one or other of the statistical categories which are used in the international classification of causes of death. If the police are considering charging someone with a crime relating to the death, the coroner is required to adjourn the inquest, and from January 1978 he is specifically forbidden to state that any individual appears to be responsible.

This fact is still far too little understood, even by professional people. As the Brodrick Committee found[1] there is still a widespread belief that coroners are mainly concerned with discovering whether anyone was responsible for a death. The consequence of this misconception is that staff in hospitals and residential homes may live in fear of a fatal accident followed by an inquest at which, they believe, responsibility for the death as a result of carelessness or error may be attributed to them. Such a fear encourages staff to take every precaution to prevent accidents happening, even if this means depriving the elderly person concerned of privacy, self-responsibility and freedom of movement. The effect of this fear can also be felt outside institutions. If a doctor or social worker refuses to force residential care upon a person whom relatives or neighbours believe to be 'at risk', threats may be made 'to report you to the coroner' if a fatal accident should occur. The fear of being blamed at an inquest can also cause hasty emergency action to be taken, especially on Friday nights and weekends, and once taken, such action is often irreversible.

Even if the professionals concerned know that the coroner is not concerned with attributing blame, they will still be aware that inquest proceedings are open to the press and the resulting report may give a slanted version of the facts. This can be especially serious when a local hospital or residential home already has a bad public image, or when a private or voluntary home depends on its public image to attract new residents. Fear of an inquest is reasonable in such circumstances and it becomes all the more important to educate press and public to understand that allowing risk can be part of a positive policy of caring. Another reason for the frightening image of the coroner's court is undoubtedly the historical antecedents of the coroner's office and the influence of old-fashioned detective stories. A further possible cause is that, for historical reasons, the language in which the inquest's findings are couched (and indeed the use of the words 'court' and 'verdict') imply an act of judgement, even though the findings have no legal implications.

The Brodrick Committee certainly believed this to be the case and said that:

> We consider it essential that a change be effected in what the public expect of an inquest, away from the attribution of blame and towards a merely fact-finding inquiry. In the long term, we can think of no more effective means of achieving this change than to abolish the 'verdict' in its popular sense by abolishing the form of inquisition and with it the requirement to reach a formal 'conclusion as to the death'. We recommend that the term 'verdict' should be abandoned and replaced by 'findings'.

As was noted above the coroner is *not* supposed to suggest any determination of civil liability or to criticise the behaviour of an individual and impute blame. However, the coroner does still have the power to attach to a verdict a rider which is designed to prevent the occurrence of similar fatalities and as the Brodrick Report points out:

> this still leaves the coroner or his jury with plenty of scope for recording riders which, in certain circum-stances, may be unfair to individuals or to public authorities. When there is concern, for example, about the circumstances of a particular death in hospital, the coroner is, at present, in a somewhat invidious position. If it appears to him that someone's conduct is blame-worthy and he says so in public, then he may, in fact, be doing an injustice to the person criticised. However, if he says nothing, then it may well appear to those close to the deceased person that the coroner is evading his duty. Our own position in this particular controversy may be simply stated: a coroner's court is not the right place from which to attribute blame and the coroner should not therefore do so.

78

The committee went on to suggest that the proper solution,

> when it appears to a coroner that there may have been
> some departure from proper standards which, if un-
> corrected, might result in further danger to individuals,
> is to suggest that he should have a right to announce in
> public and in neutral terms that he is referring the circum-
> stances of a death to an appropriate expert body or public
> authority for such enquiry and action as it may think fit.

However, all this begs the question as to whether fatal accidents in old age should normally be the subject of an inquest at all. Already, as the Tavistock Report on Fatal Home Accidents found,

> coroners do not all apply same criteria in deciding which
> are natural causes. The major discrepancy concerns old
> people breaking a leg in association with a fall. The
> fracture, which is almost invariably at the neck of the
> femur, is treated with a simple pin and plate operation
> (or less often by traction). After the operation there is a
> period of immobility during which the victim can con-
> tract bronchopneumonia, or sometimes a pulmonary
> embolism (a type of blood clot) is set up. In either case
> death can ensue, sometimes many weeks after the
> original fracture. Some coroners regard many of these
> fractures as the result of natural bone disease (i.e., the
> fracture preceded the fall rather than being caused by
> the fall) or the fracture is viewed simply as an extra
> burden on a state of chronic bronchitis and, therefore,
> they would not hold an inquest. In other cases, an inquest
> may be held and, again, evidence of predisposing bone
> disease, or chronic bronchitis may lead to a verdict of
> 'death by natural causes'. However, other coroners
> would hold inquests on all such cases and treat all such
> episodes as possibly accidental.

In consequence, the Report concludes, one coroner may return twice the number of accident verdicts made by another.[2]

These discrepancies reinforce the view expressed by the Brodrick Committee that coroners should be allowed to dispense with holding an inquest if there seemed to be no reason in the public interest for them to do so. The relevant paragraphs read:

The requirement that an inquest should invariably be held on all 'violent or unnatural' deaths has meant that some inquests are now held which, in the view of a number of our witnesses, serve little useful purpose. Several witnesses suggested that a coroner should have power to dispense with an inquest in certain cases. The British Medical Association, for example, suggested that the power to dispense should be extended to 'simple accident cases' and the Police Federation made a similar suggestion in respect of 'cases where the verdict is a mere formality. . . .' The suggestions of other witnesses varied from a proposal that the coroner should have virtually a complete discretion, to one that he should have no discretion at all. Our own conclusion, based on the evidence submitted to us and on *a priori* grounds is that the existing law is too inflexible in that it requires the coroner to hold an inquest on a number of occasions in which there seems to be no reason in the public interest for doing so. Clear cases of suicide, some deaths of elderly persons following falls at home and certain road accident deaths are most often quoted as examples of unnecessary inquests, but examples can be found within each of the categories of death in which an inquest is mandatory. We are satisfied that the only way to improve the situation is to give to the coroner what will be virtually a complete discretion as to whether or not he should hold an inquest.

We recommend that, in future, subject to three exceptions, a coroner should have a complete discretion as to the form which his enquiries may take after a death has been reported to him. In the case of the three exceptions we consider that an inquest should be mandatory. The exceptions concern:
(a) deaths from suspected homicide
(b) deaths of persons deprived of their liberty by society, and
(c) deaths of persons whose bodies are unidentified.

The Scottish system suggests that this recommendation is perfectly feasible. When a fatal accident occurs in Scotland the Procurator Fiscal is informed and he asks the police to investigate. (No autopsy is required if there are no suspicious circumstances.) The Procurator considers the police report and conducts any further investigation which he considers desirable. If the death took place in residential or nursing care, the Procurator then sees the nearest relative at a private meeting and discusses the death. In the great majority of cases, the relatives are satisfied that adequate care was provided and the case is not taken further. If the relatives, or the Procurator Fiscal himself, are not satisfied, a report is made to the office of the Lord Advocate and one of his officers decides whether a Fatal Accident Enquiry should be held. (Relatives of the deceased have direct access to this officer and may be interviewed personally by him if this seems desirable.) If a Fatal Accident Enquiry is held, this is presided over by the Sheriff and resembles a judicial Court with no-one in the dock. At the conclusion of the evidence the Sheriff makes a 'determination' which outlines the circumstances and causes of death and includes comment on any reasonable precautions which might have been taken to avoid the death and any defects in any system of working which contributed to the death.[3]

If such a system works quite adequately in Scotland, there would seem to be no good reason why a similar discretion should not be allowed in England. The consequence would be that, subject to the exceptions laid down by the Brodrick Committee, an inquest would only be held if either the coroner, or an interested third party, thought it desirable after the coroner had completed a confidential report on the relevant facts. Such a system would certainly lighten the anxiety about accidents which is now felt by care and nursing staff, and it would also be welcomed by busy professional people, such as doctors and police, who, as the Brodrick Committee found, feel that an inquest at which personal attendance is required may be a waste of time and serve no very useful purpose. However, the change might be less popular with coroners themselves. Two coroners who have been consulted both felt strongly that ceasing to make an inquest compulsory would be a retrograde step. One thought that the knowledge that a full enquiry is always made after a fatal accident tended to 'keep people on their toes' and helped to ensure a high standard of care. The other thought it was extremely difficult for the general public to get the facts about an accidental death from large impersonal institutions, such as modern hospitals, which are adept at fobbing off enquiries and complaints. If a full public inquest with personal attendance by witnesses was not the rule, he thought that relatives might believe that a cover-up was taking place. He saw the inquest as one of the few remaining opportunities for the individual citizen to obtain a personal response from faceless institutions and believed that this offered a valuable safety valve for relatives who otherwise had no means of expressing resentment or suspicion. (Both these coroners tended to minimise fear of appearing at an inquest and to assume that because *they* knew what it was all about, those who appeared before them or who might do so, would be equally well-informed.)

Neither of these objections would seem to have much validity if it remained open to the coroner to hold an inquest whenever he felt that this might be useful and if the relatives also had a right to ask that one should be held. At least, the Brodrick proposals on this point should be given a fair hearing, instead of being relegated, as they have been, to the limbo of a Home Office working party which has spent eight years in trying to draw up a discussion document based on them. Those who are concerned with the liberty of the elderly in institutional and residential care should consider political action to get this whole area of concern properly debated, with a view to revising the system. In the meantime it remains essential to educate both the public, and professional and care staff, about the real purpose of an inquest and to check whether coroners are in fact as non-judgemental in their findings as they are supposed to be. NCCOP would welcome accounts of actual experience of the system and any evidence or opinions concerning its effect on the quality of institutional and domiciliary care.

REFERENCES

1. *Report of Committee on Death Certification and Coroners*, Chaired by Mr Norman Brodrick QC, Cmnd 4810, 1971.

2. B. Poyner and N. Hughes, *A Classification of fatal home accidents* Report to the Department of Prices and Consumer Protection, Tavistock Institute of Human Relations 2T 140, January 1948.

3. *Fatal Accidents and Sudden Deaths Inquiry (Scotland) Act 1976.*

The Court of Protection

Every year the Court of Protection takes control of the affairs of a number of elderly people who are considered to be mentally incapable of coping with business. Exact figures are not available because the Court does not break referrals down by age. However, the Court believes that the great majority of those referred are elderly and this is borne out by the fact that the *average* length of time for which a person's affairs remain in the hands of the Court is five years and some of the referrals arising from subnormality, brain damage and chronic mental illness may be of quite young people with a long life expectancy. (Very few people resume control of their affairs once the Court has taken them over.) The numbers referred are going up steadily each year – 2,678 in 1975, 3,685 in 1976, and 4,045 in 1977. This increase probably reflects the rise in the numbers of the very old and therefore the incidence of confusion and dementia. It may also reflect an increase in house ownership with consequent need for legal authority to dispose of property when a person becomes incapable. About 20,000 cases are now being handled by 170 civil servants headed by two experienced barristers – the Master and Deputy Master – and four Assistant Masters who have risen through the ranks and have had long experience in handling the cases referred to the Court. Their powers and responsibilities are set out in Part VII of the Mental Health Act 1959.

Two key questions arise. Who defines 'mental incapacity' of handling affairs? And is the Court in a position to see that its clients' affairs are handled in their best interests?

The legal concept of 'mental incapacity' is certainly very vague. The explanatory leaflet published by the Court is headed 'mental patients possessed of property' but goes on to say 'many mental patients are, of course, able to manage their own affairs but some are not and it is with these that this leaflet is concerned'. The required medical certificate (given by the doctor responsible for treatment) requires him to state that 'in my opinion the Patient is incapable by reason of mental disorder as defined in the Mental Health Act 1959 of managing and administering h.. property and affairs. I base my opinion on the following ground. . . .'

However, the Mental Health Act defines 'mental disorder' as 'mental illness, arrested or incomplete development, psychopathic disorder or *any other disorder or disability of mind*', so the doctor concerned is in fact being required to say that the patient is incapable by reason of mental disorder, defined as mental disorder! He does not have to be 'approved' as competent to sign recommendations for compulsory admission to psychiatric hospital, or even be qualified as a psychiatrist, and the patient need not be under any form of psychiatric treatment. This in itself may not be unreasonable, since psychiatric hospitals are not usually the best places for caring for people suffering from dementia and geriatricians often know more about the psychiatry of old age than psychiatrists. Nevertheless, since the symptoms of confusion and disorientation can have numerous physical causes, including the over-enthusiastic prescription of drugs, it is clearly important that the referring doctor should be competent to diagnose any reversible causes of mental incapacity and there does seem to be a good case for requiring a second certificate from someone qualified in psychiatry or geriatrics, in addition to the certificate from the person actually responsible for the patient's treatment.

The degree of mental disorder is not the only factor which determines whether or not a referral is made. The decision is likely to be based on social as well as medical criteria. This is probably both right and inevitable. For example, a person may have signed a power of attorney in favour of his son when still mentally alert and subsequently become incapable. In theory the power of attorney becomes invalid and the Court of Protection should be brought in. In practice, however, most people would continue to manage the old person's affairs in these circumstances, without giving the matter a second thought, and this is only likely to be questioned if another party believes that maladministration is occurring or some major decision over property needs to be made.

Another key factor is whether the doctor or other professional concerned is aware of the way in which the Court functions and is accustomed to referring people to it. It appears that some hospitals are more likely to refer patients than others.

When a referral is made the medical certificate must set out the reasons for considering the person concerned to be mentally incapable and also information as to previous history of mental disorder; the duration of the existing disorder; whether dangerous to himself or others; whether any relative has been afflicted with mental disorder; whether capable of appreciating surroundings; whether capable of appreciating extra comforts, clothing or pocket money if it is found possible to provide them and if so at what approximate weekly rate; bodily health and prospects in life; and prospects of mental recovery.

This certificate is accompanied by an affidavit, which may come from a solicitor, or from a relative or from someone else who has full knowledge of the patient's affairs. This gives brief details of the patient, next of kin and means and cost of the present method of maintaining the patient. A Receiver (who may be the applicant) must be suggested and a Referee named who is prepared to vouch for the proposed Receiver's fitness to act. The rest of the form is devoted to a description of the property involved, and other interests or debts.

The Court then sets a day for the application to be heard and a notice of this has to be delivered to the patient stating that on such and such a day and time 'the Court will consider whether steps should be taken in your interests to protect and manage your property and affairs if it appears you are unable to do so yourself and whether . . . or some other fit and proper person should be appointed to act as Receiver under the direction of the Court'. The patient is given an address to which he can send an objection or observation. He is *not* specifically told that he has a right to attend or to be legally represented but this right does exist and is sometimes exercised. If the patient does make any kind of objection, the Master concerned would take extra care in investigating the referral and might ask one of the Lord Chancellor's Visitors to make an assessment.

If an Order is made a Receiver is appointed if the size of the estate warrants it. (For smaller cases it may be sufficient for the capital assets to be frozen and the interest remitted for the patient's use.) The Receiver may be a relative, or accountant, or solicitor, or failing these, the Official Solicitor. It used to be common for a local authority welfare officer to be appointed if the person was in a Part III home or psychiatric hospital, but with pressure of work on social workers this has become less usual. The powers of the Receiver are limited and are defined in the Order, and he is required to provide a bond which more than covers the amount of money passing through his hands. He *may* be given specific authority to deal with capital monies; make loans or gifts (including gratuities to hospital and nursing staff or allowances to relatives or other persons); grant leases or tenancies; vary the patient's investments; dispose of property or incur an overdraft. If such authority is given, the Court has to be kept fully informed as to how it is used and 'the Receiver is expected to take a personal interest in the Patient's welfare and to make proposals at any time for any improvement which can be afforded in the Patient's comfort and enjoyment'. With regard to accommodation, care and treatment 'These are matters where the Patient's own wishes, if he is capable of expressing them, must be considered in conjunction with those of his nearest relative and the advice of his medical attendant' and the Court must be told whenever a change is contemplated.

How well can the Court supervise the work of the Receivers? First, as was noted above, the Court of Protection is now handling over 20,000 cases with a staff of 170 and with the best will in the world it cannot give a great deal of attention to individual situations. A good deal of power therefore lies with the Receiver and if the Receiver is also the principal heir, as must often be the case, there must be a strong temptation to conserve assets at the patient's expense. Examples of what can happen when things go wrong have been given in an article in *New Society*. In one case an elderly woman's family resisted for three years a consultant's efforts to transfer her to a private nursing home, though the relatives were eventually over-ruled by the Court. In another, an elderly widow with depression and dementia wanted to employ a companion to care for her in her own home but her daughter and son-in-law wanted her admitted to a psychiatric hospital. The consultant psychiatrist referred her to the Court so that a Receiver could authorise the hiring of a companion and told the Court that he did not think the daughter should be appointed Receiver. Ignoring this, the daughter was appointed and the patient was put into hospital. It took a year to get the Court's decision reversed, and by that time the patient had died. (Of course, it can also happen that the patient's affairs are referred to the Court by a hospital because the hospital wants to clear its bed by getting the patient into private care and the patient is unwilling to spend capital for this purpose.)[1]

There is no doubt that the Court's officials are highly experienced and take their duties very seriously. Many of the staff stay in the Court all their working lives and their knowledge of taxation and welfare benefits may be of great benefit to the patients whose affairs they handle. Nevertheless, their lack of personal knowledge of the patient and their difficulty in making any real check on whether the patient is receiving appropriate care and full benefit from his resources, remain a matter for concern. True, an annual letter of enquiry is sent to hospitals but the replies may be quite inadequate for a proper assessment to be made.

It would seem that the working of the Court could usefully receive further investigation – perhaps on the basis of a statistical analysis of cases referred over a period and a more detailed follow-up of a sample of them. In the meantime, NCCOP would be glad to hear from those who have experience of the Court's operation and practical suggestions about ways in which it could be improved.

REFERENCES

1. J. Turner, 'Under the Lunatic Law', *New Society*, January 19 1978.

Conclusion

As the introduction to this report stated, its purpose is to encourage discussion of the very complex issues which are related to the defence of elderly people's right of choice. It would therefore be foolish to attempt to sum up neatly what has been said or to advocate simplistic and generalised reform. We need to look closely and carefully for example at the legal procedures which especially affect elderly people, including Section 47 of the National Assistance Act, the Mental Health Act, coroners' courts and the Court of Protection. We need to see exactly how the analysis and management of risk can be brought into the professional training of all who deal with old people and how other major improvements in the nature and quality of professional training can be achieved – with particular regard to communication with old people, their families and friends; caring for the dying; and the treatment of those suffering from acute or chronic brain failure. We need, as Bob Browne says, to move from an attitude of mind which says 'What can we do to help' – and lays on services to compensate for observed need – to an attitude which says 'why does she need help?' and supplies the positive and remedial treatment which will operate to restore function and improve or preserve remaining abilities.[1]

However, careful and detailed attention to necessary reforms will do little to alter the way in which old people are treated unless we can also do something to change the way in which society stereotypes its older members as 'old dears', 'OAPs' or 'geriatrics' and then uses the stereotype to treat them with patronage, infantilisation, or barely concealed contempt. The forces behind this social reaction – cultural, social, economic and psychological – deserve much more attention than they have received. One clue to the double bind in which old people are put it is suggested in a paper by Peter Marris:

> On the one hand, we tend to treat old age as if it were itself a meaningful identity – the defining characteristic of a social class, to be segregated in communities and activities appropriate to its needs. This institutionalizing of old age not only emphasizes the break with the past, but implies that the elderly are somehow to find the meaning of their lives in the fact of being old. The hobbies, pastimes, busy-work often recommended to the elderly resemble, I fear, the hollow means by which those who cannot grieve suppress the recognition of loss. But old age is not a quality of character; it is a quality of circumstance. Old Charlie is still the Charles who was top of his class, wrote passionate love letters, won a celebrated court case. . . . Old Charlie's wife is still the woman whose beautiful hair was the envy of her contemporaries, who nearly married a famous man and learned a profession she never had much chance to practice. If memory now plays tricks on them, if their legs will not always carry them where they want to go, if the famous lover is long dead, and the court case relegated to a footnote in legal textbooks, that does not make them different people, with a different conception of themselves and different attachments. It only obliges them to find new ways of being themselves.
>
> But if we impose old age on people as if it were a meaningful identity, we also talk as if it should not exist at all, as if the ideal were to preserve the identity of a vigorous middle-age to the last, to defy aging and collude in a conspiring of silence over its inevitable encroachments. This makes old age a lost cause – a gallant refusal to surrender in the face of repeated setbacks.
>
> How, then, can people make sense of their lives in old age, without either denying the reality of aging, or losing themselves in the spurious identity of a 'senior citizen'? How can they reinterpret the purposes and attachments

of an active life, so as to inform another and probably more constricted range of occupations?[2]

Marris has no simple answer, but he urges us to understand that old age is not a single crisis but a series of events which are only cumulatively critical and that we are only likely to come to terms with these changes and make sense of being old if we recognise that we begin to age almost as soon as we are fully adult and that ageing and dying are part of everyday life. Only then can we give full weight to old people's perceptions of their own identities, their situations, resources, needs and wishes and cease to impose our stereotypes of age upon them.

REFERENCES

1. R. Browne, 'The old need cure not compensation', *Community Care*, No. 259, April 12, 1979.
2. P. Marris, *Conservatism, innovation and old age* (unpublished paper) University of California, Los Angeles, California 90024.

Summary of Areas of Concern

LOSING ONE'S HOME

Physical and psychological effects of entering institutional care.
Failure to test the effect of providing maximum domiciliary services as an alternative to admission.
Inadequate social and medical assessment processes before admission.
Inadequate consultation and care during actual admission procedure.
Unnecessary admissions to hospital.
Dangers of becoming a longstay patient because of deterioration in hospital or the closing up of the patient's 'social space' in the community.
Pressures on elderly people arising from over-protective anxiety on the part of relatives and others.

COMPULSORY CARE

Wide variations in the interpretation of Section 47 of the 1948 National Assistance Act and its 1951 Amendment.
Lack of national statistics about its use.
Lack of provision for informed defence of the interests of the person concerned.
Ignorance of many community physicians and magistrates about their powers and responsibilities in the use of the Section.
Lack of any formal social service involvement.
Lack of follow-up information concerning persons removed from their homes under the Act.
Use of the Mental Health Act, sedation, simple authority, lies

about 'going for a ride' etc., as alternatives to the use of the Section to compel a person to leave his home.

FREEDOM IN RESIDENTIAL CARE

Subjection to rigid institutional rules and regimes.
Protection from risk at the cost of severe loss of independence.
Surrender of control over personal finances.
Loss of contact with the community.
Rarity of clear statements about the objectives of admission and the rights of residents.
Rarity of opportunity for residents to share in decisions concerning the running of homes.

HUMAN RIGHTS AND NURSING CARE

The authoritarian nature of hospital regimes.
Loss of choice or control concerning diet, times of sleeping and waking, use of money, escape from external noise, personal clothing, and other matters relating to identity, dignity and autonomy.
The use of cotsides and 'geriatric chairs' to immobilise patients.
Lack of concern about medically precipitating factors in accident causation.
Confusion between treatment and nursing goals for the longstay patient.

CONSENT TO TREATMENT AND 'THE RIGHT TO DIE'

Inadequacies of procedures for obtaining informed and freely given consent to treatment.
Key role of the doctor in deciding whether the patient is lucid and therefore competent to withhold consent.
Factors which encourage paternalistic decision-making on behalf of elderly patients.
The use of 'extraordinary' methods of treatment for very old or terminally ill patients and those suffering from severe dementia.

Need for better training of medical and nursing staff in the care and treatment of the dying.

The free access of relatives to dying patients.

Provision of care for the dying in their own homes.

FATAL ACCIDENTS AND THE ROLE OF THE CORONER'S COURT

Misunderstanding concerning the coroner's role.

Over-protection of old people because of fear of an inquest.

Problems arising from treating all fatal accidents in old age as 'sudden and violent deaths'.

Ways in which the system might be reformed while still giving proper protection against neglect and maltreatment.

THE COURT OF PROTECTION

Inadequate safeguards in the procedure for medical certification of 'incapacity'.

Lack of independent social assessment of cases referred.

Danger that the Receiver may conserve capital at the patient's expense.

Constantly growing pressure of work on the Court's limited staff with consequent delays and difficulty in providing adequate supervision of the patient's well-being and the Receiver's conduct.

CPA Publications in Print

(All prices are subject to a 10% charge for postage and packing)

CPA POLICY STUDIES

Mental illness in old age: meeting the challenge
by Alison Norman. Policy Studies in Ageing No.1. £5.75

Age is opportunity: education and older people
by Eric Midwinter. Policy Studies in Ageing No.2. £5.00

Triple jeopardy: growing old in a second homeland
by Alison Norman. Policy Studies in Ageing No.3. £6.00

The wage of retirement: the case for a new pensions policy
by Eric Midwinter. Policy Studies in Ageing No.4. £6.00

Councils of care: planning a local government strategy for older people
by Alan Norton, Bryan Stoten and Hedley Taylor. Policy Studies in Ageing No.5. £9.50

Growing old together: elderly owner-occupiers and their housing
by Hedley Taylor. Policy Studies in Ageing No.6. £10.50

Severe dementia: the provision of longstay care
by Alison Norman. Policy Studies in Ageing No.7. £14.50

CPA REPORTS

Home help: key issues in service provision
by Rodney Hedley and Alison Norman. CPA Reports No.1. £3.50

The hospice movement in Britain: its role and its future
by Hedley Taylor. CPA Reports No.2. £3.50

Continuing care communities: a viable option in Britain?
by David Hearnden. CPA Reports No.3. £7.50

Bricks and mortals: design and lifestyle in old people's homes
by Alison Norman. CPA Reports No.4. £6.50

Going places: two experiments in voluntary transport
by Rodney Hedley and Alison Norman. CPA Reports No.5. £3.50

Co-ordinating housing and social services: from good intentions to good practice
by David Hearnden. CPA Reports No.6. £3.50

Not a nine-to-five job: staffing and management in private and voluntary residential care homes
by Terri Donovan and Deirdre Wynne-Harley. CPA Reports No.7. £5.50

Caring for cash: the issue of private domiciliary care
by Eric Midwinter. CPA Reports No.8.   £6.50

Retired leisure: four ventures in post-work activity
by June Armstrong, Eric Midwinter and Deirdre Wynne-Harley.
CPA Reports No.9.   £7.80

Polls apart? Older voters and the 1987 general election
by Eric Midwinter and Susan Tester. CPA Reports No.10.   £7.80

Staying active: in residential homes
by June Armstrong. CPA Reports No.11.   £7.80

Food, glorious food: a review of meals services for elderly people
by Deborah Dunn. CPA Reports No.12.   £7.80

OTHER CPA PUBLICATIONS

RESIDENTIAL CARE

Home life: a code for practice for residential care
Report by a working party sponsored by the DHSS and convened by CPA
under the chairmanship of Kina, Lady Avebury.
Recommendations for good practice.   £3.00

Home ground: how to select and get the best out of staff
by Brenda Hooper. For managers and heads of homes.   £14.00

Home work: meeting the needs of elderly people in residential homes
by Judith Hodgkinson. Training manual for care staff — box set of 9 booklets.   £10.50

OTHER TITLES

Transport and the elderly: problems and possible action
by Alison Norman.   £2.00

Redefining old age: a review of CPA's recent contributions to social policy
by Eric Midwinter. CPA Papers No.1.   £1.00

Aspects of ageism: a discussion paper
by Alison Norman. CPA Papers No.2.   £1.00

Audio visual aids
by Wendy Jackson. A training resource list.   £1.00

**New literature on old age: a guide to new publications, courses
and conferences on ageing.**
Bi-monthly publication — yearly subscription. For details contact CPA at address below.

For further details of all CPA publications, please send a large self-addressed envelope to:

Centre for Policy on Ageing, 25-31 Ironmonger Row, London EC1V 3QP. (Tel. 01 253 1787.)